How to Wi

How to Win Money

at the Races

NATE PERLMUTTER

UPDATED EDITION

COLLIER BOOKS

A Division of Macmillan Publishing Co., Inc.

NEW YORK

COLLIER MACMILLAN PUBLISHERS

LONDON

For J.W.

He knew horses and people
But more importantly, himself

Library of Congress Cataloging in Publication Data

Perlmutter, Nathan.
    How to win money at the races.

    1. Horse race betting. I. Title.
SF331.P38 1979   798'.401   79-18522
ISBN 0-02-081090-3

SECOND REVISED EDITION 1979
Macmillan Publishing Co., Inc.
866 Third Avenue, New York, N.Y. 10022
Collier Macmillan Canada, Ltd.

Printed in the United States of America

This book is offered to readers for informational purposes and does not constitute either an invitation or a suggestion that readers engage in turf speculation.

NATE PERLMUTTER

Contents

Introduction

So YOU DID IT. You actually shelled out the hard-earned stuff for, of all things, a book on handicapping the horses. In your heart of hearts you know that you can't *really* beat the races, but, you figure, the book is cheaper *hashish* than the brand you've been buying at the $5 window and what the hell, who knows—maybe the book's got something.

It has. In fact, it's loaded with goodies, and what's more, they're negotiable.

A word or few, however, about the rate of exchange between you and this minor, albeit meaningful, classic.

If you purchased *How to Win Money at the Races* in the sweaty thought that Hialeah is going to make like the New York Stock Exchange to your Serge Rubinstein, forget it. You're probably a born loser. Find yourself a secondhand book dealer, palm this one off on him, and next time borrow before you buy.

On the other hand, if you enjoy a Day at the Races and, with the commendable drive that made America great, you yearn to cap said day with green silver, come along with me.

Here's a ground rule: Playing the horses should be a fun, not a frantic, pastime—but winning ain't dirty.

Another ground rule: Forget about systems. I know it's asking a lot, but you simply must be brave about it. *There are no surefire systems of government, of courting, or, alas, of handicapping*. Sure, we have a chapter, and a good one too, on handicapping systems. But it's for the betting fraternity's ninety-seven-pound weaklings, certainly not for *you*. As we painstakingly explain later on, handicapping systems are basically a means of controlling

losses (no knock intended) or, invested in modestly, a
not too dangerous makeshift when you have been unable
to do your handicapping homework.

What homework? you ask.

I'm glad you asked that question.

Chapters 1 through 8 spell out all of the basic as well
as postgraduate factors of successful handicapping. They
are, in order, the *kind* of race programmed and its relevancy to your two dollars; *the weight of the horse*, its
significance or, at times, its lack of same; the nag's *age*
and its importance to the well-being of your investment;
its *sex* and why as well as how it figures in handicapping;
its past performances as a barometer of future performances (*consistency*); the element of *speed* and when it
really counts; handicapping's oft ignored but crucial factor
of *pace*; and *class*, the great and mysterious I Am of the
world of thoroughbred racing.

These are handicapping's ponderables. They're right
there for the picking. No computers, no astrology charts,
no box tops. Just the facts, ma'am, of professional handicapping—the very same facts as brought Pittsburgh Phil
and Chicago O'Brien so many moments of sweet and
satisfying contemplation as, nightly, they snuggled closer
to their lumpy money bags.

The remaining chapters, those on systems (both handicapping and betting), the compendium of handicapping
tips (Gold Nuggets), the explanation of the totalisator
board, and the instructions for reading the racing form
should be read *after* you have rated yourself C-plus or
better on the preceding chapters. Let's put it this way.
The chapters on systems and tips, clear, concise, and
brimful with the nectar of race track sophistication though
they are, are for upper classmen. Sure, those of you who
have already cheated and made right away for the systems chapters, like the kid who starts *Lady Chatterley's
Lover* on page you know what, feel 'taint so. They're easy,
you smirk. And, smirk I, sure they are. Still, the kid who
starts at the beginning of *Lady C's* etc. and permits his
libido to come along at the pace set by Lawrence (culture
you're getting here, yet) savors more fully those pages

for which he bought the book. Same here. Read and learn my ponderables of handicapping and you'll enjoy the sweet magic of winning more profitably. For one, you'll know *what* you're doing. For two, you'll know *why* you're doing it. No small things, these.

So much for ground rules. Now for some suggestions on how to use this book.

Mark it up. Mark it up like crazy. Underline, star, and check the key factors in the various chapters. That way you'll have a quick, available-at-a-glance cram course Saturday morning before test time and H-Hour. And take it easy fingering the Gold Nuggets chapter. It's a veritable anthology of the basic rules that have been sprinkled throughout the text. You'll find yourself returning to it again and again, like it was Genesis or something. On second thought, carefully tear that chapter out, fold it neatly, place it in the inside breast pocket of your sports jacket, and sneak peeks at it in between races. It will ruin the book? Worry not. For you I can get another copy—retail.

Another thing. Supreme Court Justice William O. Douglas was the most famous hiker that comes to mind. (Lawrence, Douglas—the people you meet here!) Still, for all of the mountain lodge conviviality you and the Justice have enjoyed and for all of the books he penned and you read, when you yourself are embarking for the piney woods you'd best have a floor plan of same, else you're likely to be memorialized as a file card at the Bureau of Missing Persons. Relevancy of that interminable sentence? Buy and read, nay, buy and study the *Daily Racing Form* each and every time you plan a march on the pari-mutuels. All of the handicapping savvy you'll ever need is laid out in the pages of this book. But it's the *Form* that contains the lay of the land. In their pages you'll find the daily cast of thoroughbreds for each race at every track. What's more, it also contains all of the pertinent past performances of the competing horses, of which the means of analyzing and the techniques for successfully interpreting, are herein revealed. In short, the *Form* is a *must* accessory to a Day at the Races.

Now, boys and girls, we are ready, or just about ready, to turn the page.

The track, we have established, should be approached as a day's outing, like going to Coney Island or going on a bird-watching safari. So you didn't go in the water, or you didn't spot a Louisiana heron today, but it was good to get away and it was fun. That's the track for you, too.

Also, handicapping the races *yourself*, as distinguished from letting the green sheet or the Associated Press' selections do it for you, will provide you with the utterly personal kicks experienced by people who walk Bermuda grass barefoot. There's only you, David, and your own resources, against the Goliath, Odds. And man, the sweetness of beating the odds!

And fercrisakes, go first class. You're taking ten, twenty, fifty or more dollars with you. That ain't hay. So spend the extra buck or six bits and watch the doings from a clubhouse seat. The snazzy setting and the physical comforts of the clubhouse provide the kind of atmosphere for which the *real* you was intended. Also, and this is an important also, rent yourself a pair of binoculars. Seeing a horse race through binoculars and seeing the same race with your naked eye is as meaningfully different as observing an amoeba with and then without a microscope. With the binoculars you're going to see the horses break when the starting gate is at the other side of the track; you're going to see the captain of your fate, in the person of the jockey, make his move at the head of the stretch; and you won't have to elbow the poor guy next to you, asking, "Wha' happened, wha' happened?"

And dress up! Slacks and a smart, but not too smart, jacket for the big spenders and something chic, but not too darling, for the girls. Got your pencil? You're ready then, but first turn the page and do your homework.

CHAPTER 1

What Kind of Race Is It?

I HAVE QUAFFED a fair share of twelve-year-old stuff and soda with friends whose Italian handstitched shoes and gay De Pinna sports jackets contribute to the posh décor of Gulfstream Park's clubhouse. My friends are sophisticated men of means, men who upon being offered a stock immediately ask, "It it blue chip? Is it speculative? Does it pay dividends? How much?" Without definitive answers to these elementary questions, their stockbrokers should've stood in bed. And yet, I have observed more than a few of these crafty captains of finance continuously feeding the $100 windows without inkling number one of the basic and meaningful differences in the various types of races in which they were investing. Which races are composed of reliable blue chip competitors? Which races are run with middling talent? Which races are patently speculative because the horses competing are erratic?

The answers to these questions are actually posted in the *Daily Racing Form*, and, further, in the racing program hawked at every track. My friends—let alone the thousands and thousands of racing fans whose concerns are wages and hours rather than capital gains—have simply no concept of the dollar importance of being able to distinguish the various types of races. As a result they miss the opportunity to visit and strike up an acquaintance with the nice man behind the cashier's window.

The ensuing chapters reveal my winning handicapping techniques. Because they are written with the assumption that not all racing fans understand the important differences in the various types of races, we shall proceed herewith to provide that understanding.

There are four basic classifications of races. In ascending order of quality, they are:

1. Claiming races.
2. Allowance races.
3. Handicap races.
4. Stakes races.

Claiming races are for the least expensive and most erratic thoroughbreds and are the most frequently scheduled races. On an average there are twice as many claiming races as there are allowance races and four times as many claiming races as there are stakes races. The reason for the ratio is simple. In boxing there are just so many Muhammed Alis. There are a few more who can be rated as "contenders." Lastly, there are thousands of able pugilistic plodders who dream of fame in their fever, but face futility in their future. Similarly, in racing the stakes races are the main event. There are just so many Foregos and for every Forego there are hundreds and hundreds of able, but essentially ordinary, animals. Claiming races are for them, the journeymen thoroughbreds.

You can tell which race is a claiming race by noting the word "claiming" printed over the appropriate event on the racing program. The *Daily Racing Form* provides also this information in a revealing profile of the horses' past performances. The information appears as follows in the *Form*:

Dec 1–79^{1}Bow 1$\frac{1}{8}$ 1:55$\frac{2}{5}$ ft 5 107 10^{9}8^{6}4^{3}1^h Jockey^4 *5000*

Note the italicized numeral *5000*. This means that the race described was a $5,000 claiming race. The figure might read 1500 (at smaller tracks) and might go up to 50,000 and more (at the major tracks). The significance of the figure means one thing to the horse's owner and another to the racing fan.

To the owner the figure means that by entering his horse in a $5,000 claiming race, he has offered his horse for sale at that price. If prior to the running of the race an interested purchaser submits a purchase order to the track's racing secretary, title passes. The sale is that simple. And title passes even if during the running of the race the horse is injured and must be destroyed. That's happened! If the horse crosses the finish line "in the money," the purse goes to the "old" owner. If two or more bids are placed for the horse, lots are drawn in order to determine which bid prevails. At some tracks, anyone with the hankering and the claiming price may submit a bid in a claiming race; other tracks restrict bidding to owners who have horses stabled on the premises; and still other tracks limit bidding to owners of horses entered in the same race as the horse they seek to claim.

Claiming races are, of course, more than simply a market in which purchasers may browse and perhaps buy. The claiming race provides owners of horses of modest talent, as well as owners of horses that are barely a length in front of the man from the glue factory, with an opportunity to win purses. This opportunity is built into the nature of the race. That is, an owner of a horse in a $3,000 claiming race can safely assume that the other horses in the race are also of a $3,000 value, or thereabouts. Consequently, he has a live chance to win a purse. If an owner of a thoroughbred worth, say, $8,000 gets the bright idea to enter his horse in a $3,000 claiming race so that it will prance away with the purse, the probability that his $8,000 package of horseflesh may be claimed for $3,000 promptly sobers him up.

The system is no less meaningful to the interests of the racing fan than to the horseman. For if the owners in a claiming race have, by and large, equal chances at the brass ring, then the bettor is sure of a race the talent of which is evenly matched. To the platonic racing fan this makes for an exciting contest. To the betting man it means a fairer shake at visiting with the cashier, because there are no surprise jokers in the deck.

A final and important comment on claiming races. A claiming race, as has been said, is for the lowest grade of thoroughbreds. However, an expensive claiming race ($25,000 or more) at a major track frequently features higher-grade animals than allowance, handicap, and even

stakes races at some of the minor, half-mile tracks. This
is dollar important—how important will become evident
shortly.

The next, higher, grade of races is the allowance race.
The racing program carries the identification "Allowance"
for such races, and the information in a horse's past
performance record advising that it has competed in
allowance races will read as follows:

Apr25–78⁸Suf 1$\frac{1}{16}$ 1:46 ft 10 115 1ʰ2¹2¹2² Jockey³ *Alw*

An allowance race is one in which the weights carried
by the horses (the weights "allowed" them) are determined by the conditions of the race as drawn by the racing secretary. The conditions of the race may be such as
to allow a horse more weight or less weight based on the
number of its wins and/or the kinds of races it has won
and/or the amount of money it has won and/or the
amount of its wins or earnings within a given length of
time, etc. Weight allowances are distributed so as to
penalize with heavier weights those horses who have winning records and to favor with light weight those horses
who have had lean pickings. Presumably these weight
allowances impose a kind of horseracing parity.

Allowance races usually feature unsuccessful handicap
and stakes horses whose owners are seeking a winning
spot for them, as well as horses who have distinguished
themselves in claiming race competition. Beware, however, of claiming horses in allowance races, win though
sometimes they do. Often the owner of a claiming horse,
fearful that his horse's winning ways have caught the
admiring glances of others who may claim him next time
out, will enter the horse in an allowance race. He doesn't
intend to win, or, more accurately, he doesn't expect to
win. What he is doing is protecting his horse from being
claimed, and at the same time keeping it in racing condition until its next time out in its peer company. Not infrequently such a horse will make a poor showing alongside
the fancier company of allowance horses. This poor
showing unwarrantedly ups the odds when it returns to
the claiming races. The perceptive player will keep a

sharp eye peeled for this kind of situation and will have occasion to laugh and laugh and laugh all the way to the cashier.

Sometimes, too, a high-grade claiming horse may even be a good bet to win an allowance race. This situation arises when the conditions of the allowance race allow him a substantial drop in weight for not having won races of allowance race quality. (He may not have won them because he was busy winning high-grade claiming races.)

The next rung up in the ladder of racing is the handicap race. A handicap race is so designated in the racing program and in the *Daily Racing Form*. In the *Form* a horse's handicap experience will be shown as follows:

$$\text{Mar4--79}^1\text{G.P.}^5_8 \ \ 1:23\tfrac{1}{3} \ \ \text{ft} \ \ 4 \ \ 112 \ \ 4^34^23^11^h\text{Jockey}^9 \textit{HcpO}$$

The italicized *HcpO* means that the particular race being described was an Overnight Handicap, that is, a handicap race the entries of which had to be posted with the racing secretary seventy-two hours, or less, before the first race of the day on which the overnight handicap was run.

And a plain handicap race? This is simply a race in which the track handicapper or racing secretary assigns weights to the horses in order to equalize their chances of winning. The determination as to which horse will carry how much weight is made by him on the basis of his evaluation of the horse's ability. In a handicap race, then, the racing secretary determines the weight, whereas in an allowance race the conditions of the race determine the weight assignments.

In handicap races we find stakes horses "stepping down" in class and allowance horses "stepping up" in class.

At this point we reach the highest plateau in racing, the stakes race. Here are the counterparts of baseball's All Stars and of boxing's Heavyweight Championship contenders. Among the famous stakes races, the names of which are familiar even to the ladies of the Thursday Afternoon Garden Club, are racing's Triple Crown for three-year-olds, the Kentucky Derby, the Preakness, and the Belmont stakes. Turfdom's greats, Man O' War, Citation, Affirmed—you name them. Whatever their beginnings, they were all stakes racers.

The term "stakes" is short for sweepstakes, and its immediate etymology is traced to the stakes put up by the owners of the horses entered in the race. The winner of the stakes race takes the largest slice of the total stakes. At times a stakes race will be billed as $10,000 added, or $50,000 added, or $100,000 added, and increasingly multiples of even that boxcar figure. The term "added" means that the track is adding to the stakes a given amount of money in order to enhance the prize. These added amounts attract the owners of the nation's finest thoroughbreds to the host track, and if the equines of fleetest foot are on the premises, can the crowds and *their* stakes be far behind?

But stakes races are more than simply main-event crowd-pleasers. These are the races that provide the betting man with racing's counterpart of the stock market blue chip stock. In racing, the higher the class of horse, the more consistent is his performance; the more consistent a horse's performance, the less gamble involved in giving the man your two dollars. I have estimated that favorites win a shade over 30 per cent of the races at your neighborhood track. This 30 per cent figure includes cheap platers (race track talk for low-price claiming horses). Inasmuch as the claiming horses are the least predictable in their running ways, it is obvious that the 30 per cent win record of favorites in general includes a class of horse whose winning ways exceed 30 per cent. These are the stakes horses, and I have counted some 40 per cent of their favorites as winners.

In addition to consistency of performance, the bettor enjoys another form of security when investing in the stakes races. Because of the requirement that the owner put up a stake, the betting fan need not feel uncertain as to whether his choice has been entered in this race as a "conditioner" or "tightener," while his trainer is really aiming him for a future race. The trainer can engage in that kind of practice far more economically by placing the horse in an allowance race, which does not require a cash stake from the bossman. As sure as a player can be in racing, he is in the stakes race.

The exception clause to this handicapping policy applies to the real estate in Churchill Downs. I have seen, owners enter horses in the Kentucky Derby who, on a sunbaked, fast-as-lightning-track, might, just might, nose out Roy Roger's Trigger—with racing luck. Why is this done? So that Mr. Owner can display at the club back home a copy of the racing program published on Derby Day and gurgle contentedly as he reads and reads over and over again the name of his horse in the Kentucky Derby's Morning Line. *This* is status? Ugh.

A final and money-minded observation on stakes races. Many a professional gambler waits for a high-class stakes race and then places a substantial sum on the favorite to show. If the favorite is two to one or less, the small price doesn't faze the pro one whit. In fact, he knows that if in a stakes race the favorite goes off at two to one or less, it's just about an even money bet that it will win—let alone, show.

The return on a show bet doesn't impress you? Well, let's assume that the man who makes his living by betting purchased ten one-hundred-dollar tickets on Bandylegs to show. The horse does and the show price is $2.50 for every two dollars bet. On his thousand dollars invested, the gambler has earned $250. That's a 25 per cent return. In less than two minutes. And how's your General Motors doing?

Stakes races are noted as such in the racing program. In the *Daily Racing Form* a stakes race may be noted as follows:

Jly10–79^{7}A.P. $\frac{3}{4}$ 1.16 m 6 120 1^{h}1^{1}1^{h}3^3 Jockey^4 *ScwS*

The italicized *ScwS* means that this particular stakes race is a "scale weight stake," one in which the competing horses carry a fixed scale weight. For three-year-olds, for instance, the weight is set at 126 pounds.

These then—claiming, allowance, handicap, and stakes —are the four major kinds of races. As is now evident, the type of race being featured is of dollar importance to the racing fan. The elementary knowledge that this race is a claiming race or that one a stakes race is the equivalent of knowing that this stock is speculative or that one a safe investment. Depending on his own predilections and personality, the reader will act accordingly— but now knowingly, rather than in the manner of the species that Mr. Barnum observed are so plentiful.

There are a number of variations on these races, which may be of interest to the readers in the front row. These variations are noted in the chapter "How to Read the Dope."

CHAPTER 2

Calories and You

THE WEIGHT CARRIED by a horse consists of its equipment, the jockey's weight, and strips of lead, called slugs, placed in a "weight pad," which, in turn, is placed under the saddle. Where the conditions of the race or the type of race call for a weight in excess of the combined weight of the jockey and equipment, the slugs are used to bring the horse's burden up to the designated weight. The weight a horse is carrying is posted in the racing program. In the *Daily Racing Form* it appears as follows:

Ch.c.4,by Sire-Dam, by Sire of Dam
HORSE'S NAME *118* Breeder

The italicized figure *118* means that, in the race to be run, this horse is carrying 118 pounds.

Its weight in previous races appears in the past performance records immediately beneath this line, as follows:

Aug1–79^{4}A.P. $1\frac{1}{16}$ 1:46 ft 4 *110* 1^{h}3^{3}4^{5}4^5

The italicized figure *110* means that in his last time out this horse carried 110 pounds. Today, then, he has an additional eight pounds of weight, or as the initiated say, he is "picking up weight." Were his weight assignment 105 pounds today, he would be "dropping weight."

The big *raison d'être* of weight in racing is to equalize the chances to win of horses who otherwise would be of disparate racing ability. In days of yore, prior to the use of weights, handicaps for unequally matched horses consisted of providing the less endowed horse with a head start. By requiring this horse to run a shorter distance to the finish line than its basically more talented competitor, the chances of the horses were equalized.

As we have already seen, in handicap races the racing secretary assigns weights on the basis of his estimate of the respective racing talents of the competing horses. In allowance and claiming races the conditions of the race establish each horse's weight. The conditions may designate the horse's weight based on the number of races it has won, the kinds of races it has won, the length of the immediately preceding time span in which it has won races, the amount of the purses it has won, the amount of the purses it has won within a given length of time, or combinations of these and other related conditions. Age and sex also play meaningful roles in determining the amount of weight a horse will carry, but we will discuss these factors in separate chapters.

Before this chapter is concluded, I will utter a heresy concerning weight in racing. The heresy will issue from deep within my jeans where the jingle-jangle of the track's shekels comfort me against the mutterings of racing's elders—but later. Now for some general observations concerning specific situations in which weight figures prominently in the bettor's gross income section of Form 1040.

Weight is a more meaningful factor in a route race than it is in a sprint race. The reason for this is readily understandable if you will contemplate the effect on your own stamina, muscles, and gait of running twenty-five yards with a fifteen-pound weight and running fifty yards with the same weight. Of course, the longer the distance, the heavier the weight becomes, for readers as well as for

horses. Route races include races of a mile's distance or
longer. Seven furlongs or less is a sprint race. A furlong
is an eighth of a mile.

In a sprint race five pounds is thought to slow a horse
down by a fifth of a second, or in terms of distance, by a
length. In a route race three pounds is believed to have
the same effect.

I lay off any horse who is picking up a *substantial*
amount of weight from his last race. I figure he hasn't yet
shown that he can carry it and, if he can, he may have to
build up to it gradually. How much do I consider substantial? In a route race, I will not bet on a horse who is
picking up eight pounds and has not previously shown his
ability to carry that weight; in sprint races, ten pounds.
Conversely, if a horse is dropping a substantial amount
of weight and is not otherwise an unattractive bet, I will
lean toward him, as the drastically reduced weight may
cause him to mistake the starting gate for a launching
pad. Incidentally, the average racing thoroughbred
weighs in the neighborhood of twelve hundred pounds
and stands 15 to 16.2 hands high. A hand is horseman's
talk for four inches.

Frequently, the track's announcer and the tote board
will reveal to listeners and lookers respectively that this
or that horse is going to run with so many pounds over
the weight posted in the racing program. The reason for
this is that Ol' Debbil Weight, Lucifer's emissary to the
bad dream world of jockeys, has snared another victim.
In short, the boy has reported overweight. A fairly useful
rule of thumb is to avoid horses who are going to the post
with three or more pounds over what was assigned to
them. The reason is that the conditions of the race, or the
racing secretary in his competent judgment, have assigned the horse a fair weight. When that horse, thanks to
a dessert-eating jockey, appears at the starting gate with
a weight in excess of the originally designated weight,
you are betting on a horse who is carrying a burden over
and above the one prescribed as its fair share. Put otherwise, the conditions or the racing secretary, as the case
may be, have "equalized" the horse's chances of winning

by assigning him a given weight; the overweight of the jockey now burdens the horse with an excessive handicap. Lay off.

Here's something you can rely on. In a stakes or handicap race, the horse carrying the heaviest weight is a fair show bet. This flat statement is supported by my records of hundreds of stakes and handicap races. What you are actually show-betting is the horse who by virtue of being top-weighted is deemed by the racing secretary to be the sturdiest of heart and the fleetest of foot. Said otherwise, you are show-betting the racing secretary's own choice of the "horse to beat."

To be sure, you'll not get a fancy price, but you'll get a faster return at a more substantial rate than the sharpest trader at Merrill Lynch, Pierce, Fenner and that other fellow's store. I might add, also, that I offer this formula to the casual fan who feels the need for rules of thumb as well as to the racing scholar in whose breast reposes the humility of true wisdom—that the win choice in many a stakes race at the major tracks is a guessing game (because of the near equal quality of the two or three top favorites).

A postgraduate observation now on stakes and handicap races with relation to weight assignments. In overnight handicaps (remember HcpO?) the racing secretary has an opportunity to observe the recent past performances of the horses and can therefore reasonably anticipate the horse's condition. He can also anticipate—with an assist from the weatherman—the track's condition so that his weight assignments are likely to be realistically related to the ability of the horses to handle them. In many major stakes races, however, these factors cannot be considered because the weight assignments are made far in advance of the actual race. This sometimes results in a heavy impost on a horse who is running well at the time his owner entered him in the stakes. He gets an assignment of, say, 126 or even 130 pounds. Comes the big race and in his recent outings this horse hasn't seen a thing but tails and rumps. Still, he carries heavy weight. It ain't fair. Conversely, a horse that has been lightly raced, or has been raced for conditioning purposes, or simply hasn't found his stride, is entered in an as yet far-off stakes race and draws a featherweight. Thereafter he zips like lightning, but having already been assigned his light-weight, keeps it in the big race. This ain't fair either.

In allowance and claiming races of less than the mile distance, I just about ignore a three-pound difference of weight in those races I deem to be an investment oppor-tunity. The longer the race, however, the more attention I pay the weight factor. If my handicapping homework results in my considering two, possibly three, horses as the likely contenders in a race, and their class (we have a chapter on class) and their speed and pace (we have chapters on these too) are about the same, then a three-pound, or better, advantage held by one of the horses becomes a meaningful consideration, especially in a route race. Still, even here the weight factor will have to take its place alongside factors of consistency of performance (discussed later on), the identity of the jockey, whether or not it is a route race, and which of the horses have been raced most frequently and most recently. Note that the cheaper the horse, the more regular work it requires for winning form. Also, the classier the horse, the less meaningful is the weight factor.

In these latter comments, I have supposed the evenness of class and speed factors. If the factors of class and speed, and, in route races, pace, are not equal among the contenders, then no matter the weight advantage, forget it. Class, speed, and pace are far more important than weight. Remember that always and you'll be paid for this book many times over its ridiculously cheap price.

Having said this, let us consider a not uncommon situa-tion where a careful reading of the conditions of a race can result in a shower of coins for the racing *aficionado*. The key here is the weight factor.

Not infrequently the conditions of a race will provide weight allowances based on the claiming price for which the horse has been entered. That is, a race may be desig-nated as a claiming race for $5,000 and three pounds may be allowed for horses entered at $4,500. Got that? Hold it. Now let's proceed.

Such conditions often continue with an allowance of, let us say, three pounds for horses that have not won a race within the past month.

Obviously, then, and this bears close reading and for the racing neophyte perhaps repeated reading, a horse equal in class and speed with its competitors *who has been entered at $4,500 and who did not win his last time or two out, but was close up in races run at a faster pace and speed than the races won by competing horses who are now entered at $5,000* enjoys a substantial weight advantage. He gets three pounds off the base weight for having been entered at $4,500. He gets three more pounds off for not having won a race within the prescribed time (although he was on the pace in faster races than those the other horses won). That's a six-pound advantage, and for a horse whose class is not inferior six pounds ain't hay. A truly beautiful feature of this kind of situation is the fact that the betting public, impressed by the other horses' recent wins and higher claiming price, is going to establish them as the favorites. Thereby hangs your bigger price on the horse who in fact is the best bet.

Earlier in this discussion I indicated my semi-smirking attitude toward weight, the holy of holies in the Temple of Racing Secretaries. I am underwhelmed by the importance of weight. I think it is one of handicapping's most overrated features. Thousands of races studied have proved to me conclusively that the horses carrying the heavier weights finish in the money. Now only the simpleton in the back of the room will grin and ask, Teacher, does that mean that heavy imposts make a horse run faster?

Of course not, simpleton. What it does mean is that, by and large, the heavier the impost, the better the horse's past performance. That's why he's been assigned the heavy weight—because he's a winner. In handicapping, past performances are the true barometer of the animal's ability to repeat its form. In short, inasmuch as the better horses carry the heavier weights, and inasmuch as the more heavily burdened horses usually run in the money, weight does not in fact equalize the chances of the competitors. Otherwise those horses with the featherweights wouldn't consistently be the least supported choices and the least profitable investments.

Old-timers, their reminiscences frayed by romanticism, are already reacting to these observations with recollections of racing's counterpart to Bobby Thomson's thunderous ninth-inning two-men-out home run in the final Giants-Dodgers playoff game for the 1951 National League pennant. Racing's counterpart to that high point in baseball drama is the 1944 Carter Handicap in which three horses, Bossuet, Brownie, and Wait-A-Bit, finished in a dead heat. Time and time again this truly thrilling race is used as a testimonial to the late John B. Campbell's genius in equalizing, through weight assignments, the chances to win of three horses of disparate ability. And testimonial indeed it was! But how many times has it happened? Once. And how many times are there no less than ten or fifteen or more lengths between the winning horse and the horses bringing up the rear? The answer is simple, in almost every race on the card. Weight, no matter the hand-me-down views of so-called experts, does not in fact equalize the winning chances of horses. Light weight simply does not a Seattle Slew make of a horse that is otherwise not of Seattle Slew class.

When class, speed, and pace are about equal, then and only then does weight become a factor of importance. This kind of situation is usually camouflaged in the conditions of the race. A careful reading of the conditions is as necessary then as would be a reading of the prospectus of the company in which you plan to invest. If you are the dilettante type of racing fan and do not really intend to read the conditions (they're in the racing program and in the *Daily Racing Form*), hitch your wagon to the racing secretary and show bet the horse with the heaviest weight in stakes and in handicaps.

A final word before proceeding to age as a handicapping factor. Notwithstanding my pooh-poohing of the importance of weight, enough of the slugs *will* take their toll. I personally stay away from betting horses who are carrying 126 pounds in a route race and who haven't previously shown their ability to do so against a like class of competition.

CHAPTER 3

Separating the Men from the Boys

THE AGE OF A THOROUGHBRED is an important factor in handicapping winners. And yet, surprisingly, it is lightly considered by many racing fans. I suspect that this is due to its high visibility—it's right there in the past performances and in the racing program. Something there is about this that is too easy to be understood. Some players, frustrated mathematicians at heart, aren't fully convinced that they are being scientific unless they can play with charts, and they all but use a slide rule and calipers to measure the effect on the contenders of past weight assignments and racing distances as related to current weight assignments and racing distances. They are so busy computing, projecting, dropping fractions, and otherwise contributing to the vitality of the pencil industry that they lose sight of a very obvious, very simple fact: that the scale of weights (page 116) which racing secretaries use as a guide in assigning weights to equalize the horses' chances to win is directly related to the *age* of each horse! Evidence enough of the importance of age in selecting your equine meal tickets?

The age of a horse will appear in the past performances as follows:

Br. c. 3 by Sire-Dam, Sire of Dam
HORSE'S NAME   Breeder

The italicized numeral 3 means that this horse is a three-year-old. All thoroughbreds, like the Chinese (my,

what you learn here!), share January 1st as their birthday. A horse foaled on March 2nd and a horse foaled on
December 30th are both one year old on January 1st next.

Before proceeding to a discussion of the effect of age
on a horse's competitive performance, it will be useful to
define some relevant terms that are as meaningful to
horsemen and to players as man and boy and girl and
woman are to civilians.

Until he has reached his fifth birthday, a male horse is
a *colt*. (In the past performance lines colt appears as c.
This abbreviation immediately precedes the numeral des-
ignating age.)

On his fifth birthday the colt becomes a *horse*. (In the
past performances, h.) Horse, of course, is also a generic
term descriptive of both sexes and of all ages of the
animal. In this book, where the word horse appears,
I have used it generically, unless otherwise specified.

Regardless of his age, a male horse who has been
unsexed is a *gelding*. (In the past performances, g.)

Regardless of his age, a half-castrated male horse or a
horse with one or both organs of reproduction hidden or
missing from his sac is a *ridgling*. (In the past performances, rig.)

Until she has reached her fifth birthday, a female horse
is a *filly*. (In the past performances, f.)

On her fifth birthday, a filly becomes a *mare*. (In the
past performances, m.)

Lastly, a *weanling* is an animal newly weaned, and a
yearling is one that has passed his first birthday but is not
yet two years old. Neither weanlings nor yearlings are
raced. As two-year-olds, horses are lightly raced over
shorter distances, building up in both frequency of races
and in distances as they mature.

Horse racing being a test of speed and endurance, the
spoils of victory are destined for the horse whose stride,
muscles, and stamina combine to prevail in the grind of
competition. The physical conformation of a horse, the
potential of his muscles and of his stamina approach
optimum capacity as he emerges from "boyhood" (colts

and fillies) and enters "young manhood" (horses and mares).

Notwithstanding the color, hoopla, sentiment, drama, libations, soaring hopes and plummeting ones, too, that attend the Kentucky Derby, a three-year-old is not a fully developed horse. His conformation and stamina are not yet a match for the less glamorous, older thoroughbreds. Indeed, while horses, like people, come to full maturity at different ages, thoroughbreds generally attain their maximum development at the age of seven. (A quite outstanding exception, three-year-old Carry Back, winner of 1961's Flamingo, Florida Derby, Kentucky Derby, and Preakness, all for three-year-olds, prevailed over a field of older horses in a seven-furlong race at Atlantic City. Never you mind it. Like Alexander, who achieved The Great before he was old enough to be bored by shaving, the occasional Carry Backs of racing are the exceptions that prove the rule.)

So rare are they that I carry this reminder in my Hialeah Investment Portfolio: In races for three-year-olds and older, select an older horse if the race is a route race (over a mile). This rule will pay adequate dividends even in sprint races, but is especially rewarding in route races, where stamina assumes prime importance. (Three weeks following his victory over older horses at the seven-furlong distance, Carry Back again competed against older horses, this time at the route distance of a mile and three-sixteenths, in Atlantic City's United Nations Handicap. He lost. In fact, he ran out of the money. The naïve racing public, blinded by his past performances against his age peers, had made him a six-to-five favorite! Case closed.)

At the Florida tracks, where the flamingoes and I have a better than casual acquaintance, I go so far as to avoid *four*-year-olds in route races for four-year-olds and older. The reason is as simple as it is instructive. Florida's is a winter and early spring season. Because all horses share January 1st as their birthday, we know that a horse foaled in June will be officially one year old six months later.

One year and six months later he will be two years old, and so on, until three years and six months later, when he will officially be four years old. Consequently, a four-year-old racing against older horses at Calder in January or at Hialeah in February or at Gulfstream Park in March is not *really* four years old. At age four this may not count too heavily if he has a substantial edge in class and the race is of sprint distance. But in a route race? He is a boy doing a man's work in competition with grown men. I avoid him in route races from January through July even when he has a modest class edge, for he has neither the stride nor the stamina of his older, more developed company.

Again, as with all rules, apply it neither so hard nor so fast as to include the Olympian talents for whom there are no rules but those that they must shatter. For the thousands of remaining thoroughbreds left to the player the rule is money in the bank.

At this point the attentive reader may wonder why, in view of the superior physical conformation of seven- and eight-year-olds, one reads so infrequently of their sterling deeds on the race course. Before proceeding to additional tips on age as a handicapping factor, attentive reader warrants edification.

The stables adjoining America's race tracks are chock full of active, older horses. Their younger stablemates, however, steal the press. The reasons for this follow.

Two-year-olds are racing's debutantes. They are the crop from whose number next year's major derby candidates will stem. They are like babies in the movies. Scene-stealers. The three-year-olds are the glamorous stars of racing. They are the principals in the Kentucky Derby, racing's counterpart of baseball's All Star Game. Indeed, the Churchill Downs feature, the Preakness, and the Belmont, racing's Triple Crown for three-year-olds, is something of an extended World Series and is accordingly headlined in the sports pages of the press. Finally, last year's outstanding three-year-olds are this year's closely watched four-year-olds in the nation's major and highly publicized stakes events. All of this conspires to focus attention on racing's young 'uns. This is in the best tradition of a nation in which Françoise Sagan outsold Simone de Beauvoir ten to one.

But there's another reason for the pre-eminence of youthful equines in racing's forums. It's a business reason, one rooted in profit, which makes it, of course, most important.

The great and consequently well-known competitors among the older horses are usually withdrawn from the fray. Oh, the five-, six-, seven-, and eight-year-old horses that remain in action are more than adequate to the task of outdistancing their younger stablemates in the route races, but the great ones, the ones whose youthful exploits distinguished them, are retired. How come?

The greater the winning record of a horse and the higher its earnings, the more valuable are its stud fees. The assumption is that the progeny will inherit the class of the sire and or dam and or grandsire and or grandam. (One aforementioned Carry Back, a commoner, was an exception to prove the rule.) It stands to reason, then, that in view of the physical hazards of racing and the delicately wrought nature of thoroughbreds, an owner is risking his future income by permitting a horse that has already established his greatness to continue racing. An injury during the course of a race can well incapacitate the animal or even require his being destroyed. The stud farm offers no such problems while providing the high-strung racehorse with therapeutic amusement and his owner with dowries, dowries, dowries, and dowries. Stud fees in the four figures are common, and five-figure stud fees not uncommon. A service to Secretariat has been rumored to cost $100,000!

Apart from the possibility of injury, the fear that a horse's form may suffer reversal is enough to retire him. While his record is impressive, the potential stud fee is proportionately impressive. Should, perchance, the horse's competition improve or he himself lose that all-important desire to win, his past performance record suffers and with it his potential stud fees. Better, then, to retire the top-rated but beyond-youth's-threshold campaigner while the price is right.

So much for attentive reader.

Now let us consider a common situation in which an understanding of the importance of age in handicapping can turn up a winner, and usually at a nice price.

The race is for three-year-olds and upward. It's a claiming race at $6,000; horses entered at $5,500 are allowed three pounds. It is the time of browning leaves, October. The distance is a mile.

According to the scale of weights (page 116), the base weight for three-year-olds at this time of year is 122 pounds. Four-year-olds and older carry 126 pounds. The conditions of the race provide that non-winners of two races within a specified time preceding the race are allowed four pounds. Non-winners of one race within that time are allowed six pounds.

At this point we know that the accumulated wisdom of racing's savants suggests that in October, for a distance of over a mile, a three-year-old requires a four-pound handicap when competing with older horses. (The scale of weights' difference between 126 pounds and 122 pounds.)

Now let us assume that the three-year-old contender in this race has won two races within the specified time, and that there are four- and five-year-olds competing who have not won one race in that time. These horses are immediately allowed six pounds, and resultantly carry 120 pounds. If among this group of older horses there are some who have been entered at $5,500 rather than at $6,000, they receive an additional three-pound allowance, further diminishing their load to a weight of 117 pounds. Finally, and commonly, let us assume that one of these horses is the mount for an apprentice jockey who is entitled to a five-pound allowance. Note, now, with what you are confronted: a three-year-old with a fine past performance record and a weight of 122 pounds, and an older horse without wins within the conditions of the race but with a weight of 112 pounds. The fully grown horse, notwithstanding the scale of weight's deference to the physiognomy of youth, has a substantial weight advantage, and, to boot, the race is over a route distance!

What has happened now to the weight advantage that the three-year-old requires to be equally matched against "manlier" horses? Obviously, it has been dissipated. Dissipate too, then, the illusion of the three-year-old's past performance of two victories within the time limit. Odds are that if you look closely at its past performance record you'll find that it was against his own age peers, three-year-olds, or, if he did compete against older horses and prevailed, it was a sprint race with the weights far more evenly distributed.

It is because the casual bettor makes horses like this three-year-old into favorites that so many favorites—some 70 per cent—lose. You needn't hold win tickets on destined-to-lose horses, if you learn to separate the men from the boys.

CHAPTER 4

Vive la Différence

TRY TO THINK OF A SPORT in which males and females play, gambol, or are otherwise matched with each other. Outdoor sport, that is. The answer, for $64,000 is horse racing.

As a rule, physical sports involving strength, speed, stamina, and agility are not coeducational. Horse racing is the exception. Players reared in the city as well as near-sighted grandstand and clubhouse players can nonetheless distinguish the equine sexes through the courtesy of the *Daily Racing Form* and the racing program. In the past performance records sex is noted as follows:

Ch.c,4, by Sire-Dam, by Sire of Dam
HORSE'S NAME 118 Breeder

As explained in the preceding chapter on age, the italicized *c* means that the horse is a male who has not yet reached his fifth birthday. Thereafter he is a horse (h.). Female horses, you will recall, are either fillies (f.) or mares (m.), depending on whether they look forward to or back upon their fifth birthdays. Unsexed males are geldings (g.). Ridglings (rig.) are males who are half castrated or who have one or both male organs missing from or hidden in their sacs.

In view of the fact that most horse players are neither sophomores in veterinarian schools nor contemplating careers as equestrian matchmakers, one might suppose that there is some handicapping relevancy to this discussion. There is.

As in the case of the male bipeds who breed, train, and race them, the male quadrupeds herein being considered are endowed with physical advantages of strength and conformation over their female playmates. Indeed, the analogy between *homo sapiens* and *equus caballus* extends further.

When a female horse is in her mating period, she becomes moody and erratic. In terms of the interests of the betting public, she can be expected to perform in a manner inconsistent with her past performances. Indeed, track authorities will not permit a horse in this condition on the track. However, there are occasions when a female horse may be entering this period and even so knowledgeable a connection as her trainer may not yet have noticed it. In such case, holders of win tickets on male horses may be even worse off than the players who, ignorant of her condition, liked the filly or mares, as the case may be. The reason for this is that male horses—geldings excepted—instinctively sensing the lady's sociable frame of mind, may not wish to draw out in front of her, preferring, optimistically, to follow close behind.

The more common relevancy of sex in racing, however, is the brute physical advantage of the male. Racing secretaries compensate for this by providing weight allowances for female horses. According to the official Scale of Weights for Age, "In all races except handicaps and races in which the conditions expressly state to the contrary, 2-year-old fillies get sex allowance of 3 pounds and 3-year-old fillies and mares 5 pounds before September 1, and 3 pounds thereafter."

I really don't think this helps very much. The thousands of races I have witnessed and the many times that number that I have studied have provided me with a very simple, very profitable rule of thumb. To wit: Lay off female horses in coeducational races. The longer the race, the more steadfastly shalt thou adhere unto it. The reason? Route races test strength and endurance, and these are maledom's *forte*.

When a truly outstanding filly or mare comes along, I of course slacken the rule. Even then, however, the race will have to be for seven furlongs or less, weight assignments will have to be right, and the class of the female horse has to convince me that were she human she'd be an Amazon.

In races exclusively for the distaff side of *equus caballus*, I favor the mare against the filly. The fervor of my favor increases with the distance of the race. (Remember the last chapter, the one on the importance of age?)

Now for an illustration of a not atypical situation in which the betting public foists the responsibility of Favorite on an innocent filly or mare and in which attentive reader's loyalty to the male animal will reap rewards.

Let us assume a race the base weight for which is 118 pounds. The conditions of the race provide a six-pound allowance to horses that have not won two races within a given period of time. It is a claiming race with a sliding scale of claiming prices.

Now, assuming that the race is at Calder, which meets in December, the filly on the racing program is allowed three pounds. She's in, then, with 115 pounds. Also, by virtue of wins her last two times out, m'lady is established as the favorite on the tote board.

But let's take a closer look. There are a colt and a gelding in the race, both of fair sorts. Neither have experienced a win in their last few tries, although they have shown some improvement. Not having wins however, they are immediately in at 112 pounds. If entered for less than the top claiming price of the race, they shed additional weight. If either or both have an apprentice jockey up, still more weight is dropped.

Very plainly now, the filly who is entitled to *less* weight than the colt and the gelding, because of her weaker sex, is actually carrying *more* weight.

Unless—unlikely circumstances—her last two victories were in mixed company, over the same or a longer distance, with the same weight distribution, avoid the illusion of her being the best bet. For illusion it is. The unsophisticated public has been beguiled by her earlier victories and has consequently established her as the favorite. However, she is now carrying more weight (because of her past performances) against biologically superior competition carrying less weight (because of their past performances). The likelihood of her repeating her victories under these circumstances is no better than that of Esther Williams in a race against Tarzan. And the longer the race, the less the likelihood for both Esther and the filly.

CHAPTER 5

It's Not the Hobgoblin of Little Minds

HAD RALPH WALDO EMERSON tarried less in Boston Common and mixed more at Suffolk Downs he likely would never have opined, admittedly with philosophical merit, but with handicapping naïveté, that consistency is the hobgoblin of little minds. To the contrary, consistency of performance has illuminated Truth for many who have sought it while bedeviled by the gnawing uncertainty, "Shall I play the 4 horse, or the 1 horse? Or maybe the 7 horse?"

In racing, consistency refers to the regularity with which a horse comes up a winner or finishes "in the money." An inconsistent horse is obviously one whose past performance record is erratic and consequently unsuited to projecting the likelihood of his future form. A horse with a goodly percentage of wins, places, and shows is said to have consistency and therefore has a reliable base from which the caliber of his future performances can be projected.

What constitutes a goodly percentage? A horse that is invited to stroll around the winner's circle one time for every four times he leaves the starting gate may be rated as consistent. A horse that finishes in the money (win, place, or show) 60 per cent of the total of his starts is also fairly consistent. He warrants your consideration and possibly your two dollars.

Consistency can be determined from information appearing in the *Daily Racing Form.*

It appears in the *Daily Racing Form* as follows:

	B.h.7 by Sire-Dam, by Dam's Sire
HORSE'S NAME 114 Breeder	*1979 12 4 1 3*
	1978 14 1 2 1

The italicized figures mean in 1979 this horse went to the post twelve times. In four of these outings he won. On one occasion he finished second, or placed. On three occasions he finished third, or showed. Similarly, the second line denoting the previous year, 1978, reveals that, of fourteen times raced, this horse finished in the money four times. He won one race, placed in two races, and showed in one.

There are a number of methods in use for the determination of consistency, and the player may wish to experiment with them before settling upon any one.

Mention has already been made of the formula involving the percentage of wins and of finishes in the money, as related to the total number of starts. With this method, the seven-year-old horse in the illustration emerges as a commendably consistent animal *if* he is rated for 1979 only. In 1979 he has come home a winner in a gratifying 33⅓ per cent of the time. He has finished in the money, 66⅔ per cent of the time. For 1978 and

1979 combined, these figures fall sharply because of his unimpressive performances in ten of his fourteen '78 races.

Another fairly common method used by consistency players is to add the percentage of wins and the percentage of times the horse has finished in the money. The horse with the highest total figure is then rated as the most consistent performer in the race. In the above illustration, the horse's rating with this method would be 100. (33⅓ per cent plus 66⅔ per cent.)

Still another, and for my money wiser, method of rating consistency is to consider only the horse's last five or six races, if the first of these races was run within three months of the current race. More preferably still, if the current meeting is old enough, I will use only the horse's performances at the track at hand. The consistency percentages arrived at in this manner have decided advantages over the percentages spanning larger numbers of races and longer periods. For one, you are rating the horse on his current condition. Note the record of the seven-year-old horse that I used to illustrate consistency. A percentage of wins or finishes in the money for the combined races of 1978 and 1979 fails to reveal the currently meaningful fact that the horse has improved substantially in 1979. A rating based on his immediately preceding efforts is plainly a more accurate pointer to the animal's likely performance today.

Another advantage of limiting the time span over which consistency ratings are made is the fact that cheaper horses—claiming and allowance racers—are not as consistent in their performance as handicap and stakes racers. Upon reaching peak form, they fall off more quickly, more precipitously than the main eventers with the top billing. Consequently, a consistency rating over a period of six months might include wins earned during a peak from which they have long since fallen. On the other hand, a consistency rating based on a horse's current racing ways is more apt to reveal whether the horse is falling off from or rising toward his peak.

Some horses "like" certain tracks. A cheap plater may not show a thing at one track and, immediately he is shipped to another, zing, he can't be held back. This factor, in addition to the concern with recent performances, sees many a perceptive handicapper fool only with a horse's consistency rating earned at the track at which the current meeting is in progress.

At this juncture, some brief comments on earnings, a factor very much entwined with consistency, are in order. We shall then return to a simple yet pregnant word used in the closing sentence of the last paragraph.

A horse's earnings are, as even Alley Oop might surmise, the amount of money that he has won in purses. This information appears in the *Daily Racing Form* immediately following the consistency data. The illustration we used for the seven-year-old horse would be extended then as follows:

B.h.7 by Sire-Dam, by Dam's Sire 1979 12 4 1 3 *$11,500*
   114 Breeder   1978 14 1 2 1 *$ 3,650*

The italicized figures reveal that in 1978 the horse under consideration won purses totaling $3,650. In 1979 when its winning ways improved nicely, thank you, its purses totalled $11,500.

Players partial to consistency ratings are likely to note well the earnings line. For certainly the horse who has earned the highest amount in purses has proven his mettle and carries the credentials of a likely repeater. The earnings handicapper, like the consistency handicapper, has a variety of formulas that he employs to determine the best bet in a race. One that suggests itself immediately is the horse with the highest earnings; another, the horse with the highest earnings over the last few races or within a given period of time preceding today's race; or, another formula, also related to consistency ratings, is the horse with the highest earnings at the track featuring the meeting. Lastly, advanced math students will take any of the totals derived through the aforementioned formulas and divide it by the total number of starts made by the horse.

The horse with the highest dollar return per start becomes the choice to win.

Now, lest freshman readers of this text get the bright idea that by simply noting the consistency and earning records of the *dramatis personnae* in the fifth race they're going to have it made, let us return to that pregnant word that we left unattended six paragraphs ago.

It is true that consistency ratings and comparative total earnings are good selection barometers. It is true, too, that if you show me a horse with a high consistency rating, I will show you a trainer who isn't fooling around. But there's a catch!

It is now eight paragraphs sincs I used the flippant but carefully chosen word "fool" as a verb describing the perceptive handicapper's employment of consistency ratings.

For indeed, the knowledgeable handicapper will fool with consistency ratings and total earnings only *after* he has done his homework on speed, pace, and class. Then, if after having considered these factors he remains uncertain as to which of two horses is most likely to love him, consistency and earnings, alongside weight, age, and sex, can be used to settle upon a selection.

Mistake me not. Consistency and earning totals are okay if you are betting the same horse each time that he races over a given period of time. Over a few races he is likely to repeat the percentage of wins that in his past performances prompted you to select him in the first place. But the odds are that you are a Saturday *aficionado* of the race horses. As a once-a-weeker you are not going to be in a position to "stay" with the horse. Consequently, you must know whether he is going to win *this* race, and it means precious little to you that if he loses this time out, he'll adjust his percentages with a win next time out. Next time he's out you're going to be back at the ranch. For this reason consistency and earning totals are meaningful for any single race only when used within the context of, and alongside with, the other prime factors of handicapping.

Some final thoughts now on consistency ratings and total earnings. When they are used to pick selections without reference to the other factors of handicapping, they are selection "systems" more properly than they are handicapping techniques. They involve no consideration of the kind of race that is being run, its distance, the comparatively recent or old indexes of the horses, the weight assignments, the age and the sex of the competing horses, and most importantly, the speed, pace, and class factors. Their value as a system is augmented by the fact that the high consistency and high earnings horses are going to provide you with a fair share of winners, the reason being not that you are a mathematical whiz kid, but that these are the horses likely to be the favorites. On the other hand, you will not long be able to afford these winners, this reason being that if one selection in three wins (the winning rate of favorites), you will have fed the pari-mutuels with three times two dollars, or six bucks. The average payoff on a favorite being less than six dollars, what do you need it for?

My advice to serious students is to employ consistency ratings and total earnings when the choices have been narrowed down to two or three horses as a result of applying the prime factors of handicapping. If you must rely on consistency and earnings, that is, if you are going to use them as system, do so when:

1. You've gone to the track on a whim and have not had an opportunity to do your homework. Simply add, and you've got instant favorites.

2. A person has accompanied you. He or she (the "person" for non-sexist readers) is complaining, mystified by the goings-on. He or she is becoming a drag, but rapidly. Explain the consistency and/or earnings system to your friend and place some Treasury Department snapshots of George Washington in his or her hand. This will provide your companion with something to do and free you for making big decisions for the remainder of the afternoon.

CHAPTER 6

S-P-E-E-D

WE ARE NOW READY FOR SPEED, the first of my three prime
factors for handicapping winners. The others to follow
are pace and class. Indeed, for sprint races the speed
factor shares kingship of the money hill only with class.
Why is speed so important? Because when you are able
to determine the *real* speed that a horse has shown in his
past performances you have a rational basis from which
to project the time in which he will cover the course
today. Compare the projected times for all of today's cast
of characters, and *voila!*, you are a handicapper.

But alas, it takes some reckoning. The real speed factor
in a horse's past performance is a tease. It seems to be
there, yours for the reading in the *Daily Racing Form*;
but no, you read the dope sheets and all you've caught is
a veil, for speed requires you to court her with close
attention before revealing her true self to you.

Still, it's not difficult. It's easy and it's fun and—what
the hell—it pays too!

The following is the first of three illustrations in which
speed figures in the *Daily Racing Form:*

$1\frac{1}{16}$ miles (Name of record holder for distance at
                this track; date set; time of record.)
4th Bel   Purse. Conditions.

44234 Horse Aug 79 Sar *1:46*   122 110
44012 Horse Apr 79 Bel *1:45⅗* 120 119
etcetera
etcetera

The above illustration is representative of the *Daily
Racing Form's* introduction to the fourth race at Belmont
Park, or for that matter to the past performance informa-

tion on the horses entered in any race at any track in America. In this lead paragraph to the past performances is listed the fastest racing time in which each of the horses has covered the distance over which they will compete today. The italicized figures in the illustration tell us that the fastest time in which the horse in the top line has heretofore covered a mile and a sixteenth is one minute and forty-six seconds (1:46). The best time in which this distance has been covered by the horse in the second line is one minute forty-five and two-fifths seconds (1:45⅖). And so on, for each horse in the race.

The numerals preceding the horse's name are the chart book index numbers directing interested players to the result charts of the horse's previous races. Following the horse's name is the month and year during which he set his personal record for the distance he is running today. Then comes the name of the track on which he did it, Sar, being the abbreviation for Saratoga and Bel for Belmont. (See page 105 for a listing of tracks and their form abbreviations.) Following the notation of the horse's best time for the mile and a sixteenth are two figures. The first for the horse in the top line is 122. This means that on the occasion of the race in which he was clocked at 1:46 for the $1\frac{1}{16}$ miles, he carried 122 pounds. The next figure, 110, tells us that today he is carrying 110 pounds.

At this point it would appear that all that is necessary to select a winner in today's fourth race at Belmont Park is to compare the times of the various horses and the one with the fastest listed time over the mile and a sixteenth is the horse most likely to succeed. On the basis of the respective times of the two horses used in the illustration it would appear that the horse in the second line can be expected to cross the finish line three lengths in front of the horse in the top line—three lengths, because the time in which the average race horse runs the distance of a length is one-fifth of a second. Inasmuch as the horse in the top line covered $1\frac{1}{16}$ miles in 1:46, and the horse in the second line in 1:45⅖, the difference in their time is three-fifths of a second. These three-fifths of a second, then, converted into distance, equals three lengths.

If all things were equal, we could stop here and avail ourselves of speedways, shortcuts, and inattentive traffic cops, as we hasten to the track to offer our financial support to the horse with the fastest time listed in the form. But all things are rarely equal. Right?

For instance, just as it is a racing truism that a fifth of a second in racing time equals a length of distance, there are other relevant truisms. To wit, in a route race, three pounds of additional weight will slow a horse down a fifth of a second. In a sprint race the same effect is assumed to result from five pounds.

In our illustration the horse in the top line ran his best mile and a sixteenth carrying 122 pounds. For today, he is shedding twelve pounds. At the rate of three pounds per fifth of a second, we may assume that the twelve pound drop in weight will result in the horse's shaving $\frac{4}{5}$ of a second from his previous best time. (If three pounds equals $\frac{1}{5}$ of a second, twelve pounds equals $\frac{4}{5}$ of a second.) At this point, then, all other things remaining equal, we can project a time of 1:45$\frac{1}{5}$ seconds for the horse in the top line in today's effort.

The horse in the second line, racing but one pound lighter than in April, 1979, when he was clocked for the distance in 1:45$\frac{2}{5}$, enjoys no statistically significant loss in weight. As a result, based on the information now before us, we can project him at the same 1:45$\frac{2}{5}$ time. Our result? The horse in the top line, notwithstanding his apparent slower time in the past performances, is really a fifth of a second, or a length faster.

Now let's look at the second of the three speed factors featured in the past performances.

Mar 9–78^{3}GP 1$\frac{1}{16}$ *1:45$\frac{4}{5}$* ft 7 118 1^{1}1^{2}2^{h}3^4

The italicized figure *1:45$\frac{4}{5}$* tells us that the *winning* horse in the third race at Gulfstream Park on March 9, 1978, was clocked for the mile and a sixteenth, at one minute forty-five and four-fifths seconds.

Now note, too, that I have italicized the numeral 3 under the numeral 4 that is perched over the 3's right shoulder. This means that the horse whose past performance record we are illustrating crossed the finish line third, four lengths behind the winner (the winner having been clocked at 1:45⅘).

Keeping in mind that one length equals one-fifth of a second, we can easily estimate the time in which the horse under consideration finished the mile and a sixteenth. That is, having trailed the winning horse over the finish line by four lengths, we add four-fifths of a second to the winning time of 1:45⅘ seconds and arrive at a time of 1:46⅗ seconds for the horse in the illustration. (1:45⅘ plus ⅘ equals 1:46⅗.) Easy? Reread it. It really is easy.

A quick review now before proceeding. A fifth of a second equals one length. To determine the time in which a non-winning horse covered the distance in a previous race, look for the winning time in the past performance lines. Let your eyes move along to the right and pause at the numeral denoting his position at the finish line and the number of his lengths behind the winner. For each length by which he trailed the winner, add one-fifth of a second to the winner's time in order to arrive at the non-winner's time for the distance. Also, in a route race, for every three pounds a horse either drops or gains, add or subtract, as the case may be, one-fifth of a second to or from the time in his past performance record. The result is your projected time for the horse's performance today, at the same distance, and with the same track conditions.

Before continuing to a discussion of other factors that require consideration in speed handicapping, an understanding of speed ratings, the third of the three speed factors featured in the past performances, is necessary.

The following is an illustration of a speed rating as it might appear in the *Daily Racing Form*:

Apr 2–78⁵G.P. 1⅛ 1:49 ft 4 114 5⁴5³3¹1¹ Jockey Alw 89

The italicized numeral 89 is the horse's speed rating.

The *Daily Racing Form* defines the speed ratings as being "based on a comparison of each horse's running time with the track record established prior to the opening of the current meeting. The track record receives a standard rating of 100. Thus a horse equalling the record receives a rating of 100. One point is deducted for each one-fifth second slower than the track record."

The illustration tells us that on April 2, 1978, the horse under consideration ran the mile and an eighth distance at Gulfstream Park (G.P.); that he won by one length (1¹); that his winning time was one minute forty-nine seconds (1:49); that inasmuch as his speed rating was 89, he ran the 1⅛ miles eleven-fifths of a second slower than the track record prevailing at the beginning of the racing meeting. This latter information is deduced by subtracting 89, his speed rating, from 100, the track record. The remainder, 11, is multiplied by a fifth of a second, giving us eleven-fifths of a second. And, indeed, Gulfstream Park's track record for the mile and an eighth is 1:46⅘ seconds, set by General Duke and tied by Day Court (1:49 less 1:46⅘ is 2⅕ seconds, or eleven-fifths).

The importance of this information? It tells us at a glance whether the horse we are considering was intended for a more socially productive profession, like pulling a milk wagon (speed ratings in the fifties), whether the horse is a fair sort (seventies and low eighties), or whether he earns his keep and then some (eighties and nineties).

The handicapping significance of speed ratings in the past performances frequently exceeds the meaningfulness of the position and the number of lengths behind the winner a horse may have finished. For instance, the past performance line of a horse may tell us that his last time out he ran seventh, some eight lengths off the winning pace. Pretty bad, huh? However, his speed rating may well be a sharp 88. This tells us that the race in which he ran seventh was a very fast race, featuring some fancy company. It suggests to us that notwithstanding his poor showing in that race, the horse can run, and if his company today is not quite as high tone he may merit our attention and our two dollars.

In addition, speed ratings can give the horse player a sense of security. Late into Friday night the player has furrowed his brows, chewed four cigars, and lost track of time while doping out Saturday's form. There's this horse that he likes, but his time for the mile is unimpressive. In fact, it's lousy. Enter the speed ratings. If the other horses in the race have earned speed ratings in the neighborhood of the speed ratings of his choice, the handicapper knows at a glance that unimpressive though the time of his horse is, it is nevertheless probably among its peers. In short, take a cupful of speed ratings, add arithmetic, and look, mom, instant handicapping! Well . . . sort of.

Parenthetically, a horse boasting a speed rating of 101 tells us that he bettered by a fifth of a second the speed record prevailing at the track prior to the current racing meeting (season). In such case, and on the assumption that during the course of the meeting no other horse betters his time, the following meeting will feature his time as the basis of 100 from which all other speed ratings for the distance will be computed.

But for a single remaining arithmetical exercise we are now ready to ascend to speed handicapping's next plateau. There all may view—and some hopefully heed—those secrets of speed handicapping, mastery of which distinguishes horse playing's priesthood from its laity.

First that exercise in basic arithmetic. In discussing a horse's time for a given distance we learned that consideration of the weight it carried and the weight it will carry today are requisite to our projections. We observed that a difference of five pounds in a sprint race and of three pounds in a route race are enough to change a horse's time by a fifth of a second. These factors are at work as well, in projecting speed ratings.

Here's how. Let us say that last week a horse ran the mile distance carrying 112 pounds, and earned a speed rating of 84. He won, and the conditions of today's race over the mile require him to run with 118 pounds. In projecting his speed rating for today, based on the information before us, we would rate this horse as a potential 82. What we have done is to shave one point from his speed rating for each three pounds of weight he has picked up. Having a burden six pounds in excess of his last outing, we project him at a speed rating two points lower. Had the horse been entered in a race the conditions of which

permitted him in with a feather, we would have added
one point to his speed rating of 84 every three pounds he
dropped.

Now, you apprentice handicapper, you, give me your
hand whilst we climb to aforementioned plateau.

Until this point, what we have done in this chapter is
to lay out the basic rudiments of speed handicapping.
Used as is, and in the absence of such modifying factors
as track conditions and post positions, these principles are
adequate to the selection of a fair amount of winners.
Used as is, their greater service, however, is in saving the
horse player money by eliminating from his selections
hopeless horses that might otherwise have seemed like
attractive investment opportunities. Still, and notwithstanding Ben Franklin's pap about a penny saved being a
penny earned, the player who saves money in nine races
by avoiding bad bets does not necessarily earn money.
Most races have three or four live contenders, and it is
the ability of the player not only to avoid *a* loser, but to
select *the* winner that earns him his penny. Or, said otherwise, speed handicapping's real pay-off relies not so much
on arithmetical formulas as it does on the knowing and
sophisticated application of basic rules. Following, then,
are some helpful hints, some blinking red lights, and some
personal prejudices designed for the remunerative application of speed factors in handicapping.

The business about adding or subtracting to a horse's
projected time fifths of a second, and adding or subtracting points to speed ratings depending on the weight the
horse is carrying today as compared to the weight it
carried before, is so, *but*—

Remember my saying in the chapter on weight that its
importance frequently underwhelms me? Well, when a
horse is showing improvement in each of his last two or
three races, three additional pounds over a route or five
additional pounds in a sprint will not necessarily slow
him down meaningfully, and may not even slow him
down at all! Similarly, a horse that has shown that he is
slumping will not necessarily get that added zing back
from a small drop in weight. The point is, avoid blind

adherence to the arithmetical formulas we have discussed. When an animal is obviously coming into its peak condition it will perform zestfully, and additional pounds will hardly be noticed by it. Conversely, when the past performance lines reveal a horse to be falling off from its top condition, shedding a few pounds of weight is no Geritol for its tired blood. Use the tested and proven formulas, but apply them with common sense rather than with horse sense.

I pay solemn respect to speed factors in sprint races. The pace factor, which is so crucially important in route races, does not figure as prominently over the shorter distances. Why? Because, as with boys running the fifty-yard dash in the neighborhood school yard, the sprint race is virtually a matter of pure speed. The route race, like the mile race in track events for our own species, involves speed all right, but speed inextricably involved with questions of pacing, intelligence, and "heart." True, to some extent these factors are at work in both the school yard sprint and in the race track sprint, but not to the same extent that they figure in the longer races.

Consequently, and this is a key rule for speed handicapping, *when the race is at seven furlongs or less, and where the speed ratings of the competitors were earned at the same track over which they are racing today, and were for the same distance and track conditions over which they are racing today, speed rating handicapping is by itself a very sound basis for investment.*

If, however, a horse got off to a bad start or ran into traffic problems, his speed figures for that particular race should not be considered. You can't compensate for bad racing luck in your arithmetical projections.

Also, if the past performance lines tell you that the horse was in over his head his last time or two out, that is, that he raced with classier horses, the speed factors for such races should not be used for projecting purposes. The horse's trainer may have placed him in these races in order to give him some needed exercise, to tighten him up while aiming him for a future race that he hopes to win. The manner in which the jockey was advised to pace the animal in this kind of race will differ from the manner in which the horse will run today's race. Therefore there is no real basis from which to project such a horse's speed performance for today.

Beware, too, of attempting to project the time established by a horse over a distance that is different from the one he is being called upon to run today. Races of different distances are run differently, and the time a horse establishes over six furlongs can no more intelligently be projected to the mile and a half distance than we can project the time of a collegian's one-hundred-yard dash to his anticipated time for the mile. Let alone factors of pace that are involved, there are the factors of stamina and courage, which are more directly put to the test in the longer race and which simply defy being projected from the shorter, less trying distance.

In addition to the danger of projecting anticipated time from a sprint to a route race, there is the danger of attempting to project speed ratings earned at past sprint races to today's route race. My promptings for this caution rest within the very nature of speed ratings. The record for the seven-furlong distance at a given track may be a very, very fast one. As a result, none but the exceptionally fast sprinters will be running close to it and to its base of one hundred. This in turn results in comparatively low speed ratings for otherwise fine horses who have raced the seven furlongs at this particular track. However, the very same track may have a middling track record for the mile and a sixteenth. This results in a situation wherein many a horse with consistent racing performances will sport a relatively low speed rating for his efforts over seven furlongs and a relatively high speed rating for his efforts at the mile and a sixteenth. So it is that we repeat: When the race is at seven furlongs or less, and where the speed ratings of the competitors were earned at the same track over which they are racing today, and were for the same distance over which they are racing today, speed rating handicapping is, by itself, a very sound basis for investment.

The single remaining clause in our key rule that remains to be discussed is "and where the speed ratings of the competitors were earned at the same track over which they are racing today." The difference in tracks can be a meaningful explanation of why a horse with a superior speed rating will trail one with an inferior speed rating across the finish line. Track records for identical distances vary. A major track will likely boast records for its various distances that were established by the nation's foremost thoroughbreds. Naturally. The major tracks, offering as they do the major purses, attract the major talents. On the other hand, the various half-mile tracks that bring thoroughbred racing to the hinterlands of America sport track records that are comparatively slower. The result is that the past performance lines of Horse A who has been running at Santa Anita or Saratoga, where major stakes are featured, will likely reveal somewhat lower speed ratings than Horse B who has been running close to the records established at some small track with corresponding racing talent. When Horse A, whose speed ratings hovered at 88 at Hialeah, meets Horse B, whose speed ratings were in the vicinity of 92 at Sunshine Park, don't you be one of those who contribute to making Horse B the favorite because you have looked at but have not really understood his speed rating. You can safely assume that although Hialeah and Sunshine are in the same state, the records at Hialeah are faster than those at Sunshine and consequently Horse A's 88 is not necessarily slower than Horse B's 92.

When I am confronted with horses who have raced at major tracks and are today pitted against horses who have raced at the half-mile tracks. I add four, or even five, points to the speed rating of the horse who has been racing on Broadway before I start comparing his likely chances against the one who has been playing summer stock.

I might add here that eastern tracks are usually deeper and therefore slower than those on the west coast. If you are handicapping in California, subdue your California

chauvinism and add a point to the speed ratings of the
eastern equines. If you are handicapping in the east, go
right ahead and indulge your back-East chauvinism and
subtract a point from the speed ratings of the visitors from
out west.

The track at which you are handicapping is not only of
relevance to the speed rating factor but to the time factor
as well. As we have just learned, a track can be relatively
deep or hard, and consequently the same horse will run
the same distance at a slower or faster time, depending on
the surface of the track. Not only do tracks vary amongst
themselves in this regard, but in some instance a single
track will be faster or slower from one to another year.

Real gone players study track curvatures. Also, the
number of turns a track requires a horse to negotiate in
order to cover a given distance is a matter of relevance.
Obviously, a turn takes its toll in speed, while a straightaway race is a faster run race.

Another track factor that plays an important, albeit less
esoteric, role in speed handicapping is the condition of
the track. Was it fast? Was it muddy? What condition
was it in? It is necessary to keep abreast of racing publications not only to study current "track equalization
charts" so as to compensate knowledgeably for a horse's
time at a slower or faster track, but also because the
condition of the track over which a horse has raced is
cited in the *Daily Racing Form* as follows:

July 10–78[1] Suf ¾ 1:16 *hy* 18 114 4⁴8¹⁰10¹²10¹⁸

The italicized *hy* signifies that the condition of the
track on the occasion of this particular race was heavy.
The various classifications for the condition of a track
include: fast (ft), good (gd), slow (sl), sloppy (sy),
muddy (m), and heavy. In races on the turf, or as it is
also called, on the grass, the track is described as being
either firm (fm) or soft (sf). In addition to being described in the past performance lines, the condition of the
track for each race is posted on the tote board. This is
done for the benefit of the betting public, which includes

handicappers who know that some horses run better than others, and others below their personal par, when the track is "off." (See page 93, "How to Read the Dope," for detecting the good mud runners.)

Some additional hints now:

Speed ratings and time-clockings of a few months vintage are not too meaningful, as the horse's condition and likely potential is more accurately revealed in his recent efforts.

When computing the time of a loser who has trailed the winner by ten or more lengths, do not assume that your figures have on-the-nose accuracy. For one thing, there is the difficulty of measuring with precision large spaces separating speeding horses. For another, a jockey will see in the stretch that his mount's cause is a hopeless one and often, rather than drive the horse all the way and unnecessarily wear him down, the boy will ease the animal up. So it is that for horses that have trailed 'way, 'way back you may feel free to add a few points to their speed ratings and drop a few fifths of a second from their time in projecting their likely doings today.

At this juncture of our text, one Dogpatch reader might well say to another, "As any fool can plainly see, speed is impawtant." And his neighbor will reply, "Ah sees!"

For indeed, speed is of prime importance. In determing the real speed that the contestants have shown themselves capable of, we are selecting the likely contenders. Unfortunately however, among the many who have grasped the significance of speed as a handicapping factor, there will be some who will hastily assume that speed handicapping is adequate by itself for selecting winners. There are some of these in every class. They are gratified by their mastery of the arithmetical formulas, recall some of the hints and some of the cautions necessary to the knowing application of the basic rules, and feel that they needn't burden themselves with additional handicapping baggage. These are the Dogpatchers who, upon being told that any fool can plainly see, promptly boast that they do.

But speed must be jointly considered, as we have purposefully iterated and reiterated, with pace and with class. And to dramatize the dead seriousness of this injunction, let me add that where class and pace combine to point to a selection with a *slower* time in his past performance than the selection based on speed handicapping, alone, I lean to the slower animal!

So, now, let us proceed to Pace.

CHAPTER 7

The Race Is Pace

THE STORY ABOUT PACE and the immortal Whirlaway is told over and over again. It makes its point and so bears repeating here.

As a three-year-old the spectacular colt could run a quarter-mile (and not just the first quarter) in twenty-two seconds! That, readers, is speed. Indeed, were Little Orphan Annie to have paused from her damn busybodying to visit the track, grow up some, and see Whirlaway in motion, she'd have filled an entire Sunday comic section with *"Leapin' Lizards!"* Unfortunately for the Calumet Farm, however, there were no quarter-mile stakes in which they could enter their miracle horse. This left them with two alternatives. One, they could recommend to, plead with, and threaten race track associations about featuring stakes races with handsome purses at the two-furlong distance and in that way cash in on Whirlaway's blazing speed. (They didn't.) Or, inasmuch as Calumet is as blessed with sanity as it is with wherewithal, they could pace Whirlaway so that when he reached the final quarter of the race, which is the quarter that counts for winning, he would have enough remaining stamina to produce his remarkable speed.

The year was 1941, and prior to the Kentucky Derby the late Ben A. Jones entered Whirlaway in Keeneland's Blue Grass Stake. But alas, the boy who had the mount permitted Whirlaway to burn up his crazy speed before the colt covered three-quarters of a mile. At that point, the pace did what weight could never do to Calumet's speed demon. He petered out and lost ignominiously.

Came the following week and the Derby Trial at time-honored Churchill Downs. Whirlaway, as in the Blue Grass Stake, was again the favorite, again heavily so. Again the boy permitted him to go all out, and again the colt's unbridled speed wore him out in the third quarter.

By Kentucky Derby time, Jones had had it up to here and gave the mount to Eddie Arcaro. Arcaro, eight feet tall in the talent department, had an instinctive feel for pace second to none in the business. To the accompaniment of sinking hearts, he permitted Whirlaway to tally along some sixteen lengths off the pace for fully half a mile. Then, ready to close, Arcaro let Whirlaway go in the final turn. And Whirlaway went! In one of racing's blood-pumpingest drives, the game colt was clocked in the final quarter of the mile-and-a-quarter route at twenty-four seconds! Naturally, he won. Not so naturally, he won by eight lengths.

The lesson to be derived from Whirlaway's performance in the Blue Grass Stakes and the Derby Trial on the one hand, and in the Kentucky Derby on the other, is one of pace. In the former races, he set a faster pace, finished at a relatively lower time, and lost. In the Kentucky Derby, Arcaro permitted his mount's supporting cast to set a slower pace, the finish time was relatively faster, and our hero won.

We see then that time and pace are not the same, and for handicapping purposes are significantly different.

The time of a race is that amount of time that has elapsed between "They're off!" and the moment in which the winning horse crosses the finish line. The pace of the race is the rate of speed at which the race itself was run. Said otherwise, the pace of the race is the running time at which the various quarter poles are reached by the horse then in the lead. For instance, Horse A may be clocked in the lead at the first quarter call. By the time the second quarter pole is reached, Horse B may be leading. In terms of assessing the pace of the race at this point, the time at which Horse A sped by the first quarter pole and the time at which Horse B moved past the second quarter pole constitutes the pace at which the race is being run. If four different horses were to hold the lead at the various quarter calls of a mile race, the pace of the race would then have been contributed to by all four horses. Of course, the final time of the race is established by the winner only.

With this distinction between time and pace in mind, it becomes evident that a fast quarter-mile or half-mile does not necessarily mean that the race is going to be a fast race, the reason being that it is not at all unlikely that the horses setting that fast pace may burn themselves out come bringing-home-the-bacon time.

In the Official Result Charts as published in the *Daily Racing Form*, the pace at which races have been run appears centered immediately below the account of the performance of the last horse in the race. (See page 93, "How to Read the Dope.") For a mile race, this information might appear as follows:

Time .23⅗, .48⅘, 1.14, 1.41. Track sloppy.

The numerals represent the time in seconds and minutes of the first horse at each position clocked. As we have seen, the first call of .23¾ seconds is the time at which the then lead horse passed the first quarter pole. The fact that that horse may have sat down to contemplate his fetlock immediately thereafter and may have never even finished the race does not in any way affect .23¾ seconds as being the pace of the race as of the quarter call. And so on for the rest of the calls.

The past performances of the *Daily Racing Form* provide pace information. A segment of a past performance line with pace data as it might appear follows:

28Sep78–2Bel sly 7f *.23 .46$\frac{3}{5}$ 1.24$\frac{1}{5}$* Clm 9000

The italicized figures represent the quarter time (.23), the half time (.46$\frac{3}{5}$), and the final time (1.24$\frac{1}{5}$) of the seven-furlong race being described.

The handicapping significance of this information is best described by illustrating and comparing the pace of two different races.

18Aug78–8 Atl fst 1 $\frac{1}{16}$ *.47$\frac{1}{5}$ 1.12$\frac{2}{5}$ 1.44$\frac{1}{5}$*
3Jun78–6 Del fst 1 $\frac{1}{16}$ *.46$\frac{3}{5}$ 1.11$\frac{4}{5}$ 1.45$\frac{1}{5}$*

Before discussing the meat in this example of handicapping the pace factor, it is well to note the slight differences in the past performance lines as they appear here. The top line tells us that on August 18, 1978, in the eighth race at Atlantic City, on a fast track, over the mile and a sixteenth distance, the pace of the race was .47$\frac{1}{5}$ seconds at the half-mile and 1.12$\frac{2}{5}$ seconds at the three-quarter pole; and 1.44$\frac{1}{5}$ seconds was the final time of the race. Our illustration is a segment of a *Racing Form* past performance line.

Now to the facts, ma'am.

In the race described in the top line, a three-year-old filly won the event. The time of 1.44$\frac{1}{5}$ is, then, her winning time. In the race described in the bottom line, a three-year-old gelding placed, half a length behind the winner. Consequently, for our purposes the winning time of 1.45$\frac{1}{5}$ is his time.

At this point it would appear then that the filly is a faster horse. Indeed, over a mile and a sixteenth, the filly would appear to have a five-length advantage over the gelding. (Remember our arithmetical formula in which a length equals a fifth of a second?)

But is this really so?

In comparing the half-mile calls we note that the pace of the race in which the gelding ran at the half-mile was fully three-fifths of a second faster than that of the filly's (.47$\frac{1}{5}$ less .46$\frac{3}{5}$ equals $\frac{3}{5}$). At the three-quarter-mile call the gelding's race still exceeded the filly's in pace by $\frac{3}{5}$ of a second. Finally, at the finish line the filly's time betters the gelding's by a full second.

But it is safe to assume that, had the pace in the filly's race been that of the pace in the gelding's race, the outcome, final timewise, would have been quite different. Indeed, were the two horses pitted against each other, the respective paces of the illustrated races tell us that the gelding would very likely have won. Why? Because the pace of the race in which he was clocked at 1.45½ was a substantially faster pace than in the filly's race. We can assume then that had the filly run her race at the pace of the gelding's race, in the final quarter she would have been a pooped little girl, indeed.

Now to put the icing on this very salient handicapping lesson. Were we to have extended the illustrated past performance lines as they actually appear in the *Racing Form* before me, the filly would be revealed as having been clocked at 1.44½ in a $4,250 claiming race! The gelding is a handicap and stakes racer of substantially higher class and has earned purses at this writing six times those of the filly! Which horse is the faster horse?

Ergo our lesson is: Final time is important, yes. In a sprint race, it's very, very important. In a route race, however, it must be considered in conjunction with pace. The faster the pace of the race, the classier the animals. Look for the pace factors and you'll likely find the animal with class. Find the animal with class and you've discovered the glory road to successful handicapping.

A horse that is "on the pace" is one that is within striking distance of the pace-setter; a horse that is "off the pace" is some lengths behind the pace-setter. A horse that can stay on the pace is always a contender.

At this point we are ready for some useful, very profitable tips in connection with pace handicapping. Indeed, I know of no way by which players can come up with more longshot winners than by a study of the pace factors in the past performances. Study speed only or class only and you will find your share of winners. Generally, however, they will be favorites or just about favorites. There's money in this, but not of scads porportions. Study the pace factor and you'll find winners—but ah, such winners!

Why so? Since pace is frequently camouflaged, the betting public, neither seeing nor hearing its message, permits itself to be Pied Pipered by low-paying favorites. The happy result is that there are fewer people to share in the pot when our longshot romps home.

Let's now consider the following past performance lines of Horsey Horsey:

Oct10 $1\frac{1}{16}$ 1:47$\frac{2}{5}$ ft 6 110 $5^7 5^3 4^2 5^6$
Oct5 $1\frac{1}{16}$ 1:49 ft 11 110 $4^5 4^3 3^3 3^3$
Sep30 $1\frac{1}{16}$ 1:49 ft 12 110 $6^6 6^7 5^8 5^6$

In applying the handicapping factors of pace for the purpose of determining whether Horsey Horsey is worth an investment, we note that three races ago, on September 30, this animal came into the stretch in fifth position, fully eight lengths off the pace. Whether his having crossed the finish line six lengths behind the winner was due to his having rallied mildly or whether it was due to the tiring of the front-running horses is not evident.

His next race helps us understand Horsey Horsey better. On October 5th we see that he remained on the pace throughout the race, finishing in the money and, even more significantly, only three lengths behind the win horse. The horse was improving—so much so that in his last time out, on October 10th, the betting public took note and supported him to the point where his odds dropped from 12 and 11 to 1, respectively, to 6 to 1.

But alas, he disappointed his supporters. After coming into the stretch but two lengths off the pace, he finished fifth again, and again six lengths behind the winner. The holders of win tickets on Horsey Horsey sighed, tore them up, and forgot him. Likely, they thought, his October 5th race was a fluke performance, or maybe that was his best and he had nothing better. In any event, Horsey Horsey is believed to have fallen back to his September 30th form.

But has he, really?

A careful scrutiny of this animal's past performance record as depicted in the illustration actually reveals that he is *still* improving! In fact, had he run as good a race on September 30th and on October 5th as he did on October 10th, he would have won both times!

Sure, Horsey Horsey finished fifth, six lengths off the winner's pace in his last time out. However, note the final time of the October 5th and the September 30th races. It was 1:49. On September 30th, Horsey Horsey's time was 1:50⅕ (one-fifth of a second added to the winning time of the race for every length behind the winner). On October 5th, improving, he crossed the wire in 1:49⅗. Then, on October 10th, when it appears that he fell back to his September 30th form, we note that the winning time of the race was 1:47⅗. Horsey Horsey's time was 1:48⅘! (Add six-fifths seconds to the win time.) What's more, after a not so hot break from the starting gate (fifth, seven lengths off the pace), Horsey Horsey came along beautifully until he was but two lengths off the pace in the stretch. Two lengths off the pace, we must add, in a substantially faster race.

In short, Horsey Horsey is decidedly on the move. In his last race he was in over his head. Today, the betting public, feeling it has been burned by him once, will avoid him. Don't you, for today his trainer will likely have placed him right, and his odds will return to the neighborhood of eleven to one.

Were I not a mild sort of fellow, given to Jimmy Stewart-like understatement, I would have used bold, capitalized lettering for this discussion of Horsey Horsey. For its lesson is of paramount importance to successful handicapping. In order to wind up a meeting in the black, the betting fan must have selected a few long-shot winners. A .333 batting average, as it were, will likely see the player break even or drop a small amount. It's the few long shots that make the difference between a winner for the season and a guy who says he was a winner. And it's attentiveness to the pace factor that can give the player membership in the former, elite club.

And so, *watch for the unimpressive horse who in his last time or two out showed his ability to get on the pace as he came around the far turn into the stretch.* It's a sign that that horse may be improving. Never you mind that he faded before the finish. Unless his past performance record reveals him to be a quitter, his having come on in the stretch may well be a tip-off that next time out he will be ready to go all the way.

A caution, before we leave pace and hold forth on class.

A horse may show marked improvement in his ability to stay on the pace, but may, in fact, be a bad bet. This can best be illustrated by repeating the past performance lines for Horsey Horsey, with some slight but telling variations.

Oct10 $1\frac{1}{16}$ 1:49 ft 6 110 $5^7 5^3 4^2 3^1$
Oct5 $1\frac{1}{16}$ 1:47$\frac{2}{5}$ ft 11 110 $4^5 4^3 3^3 3^3$
Sep30 $1\frac{1}{16}$ 1:47$\frac{2}{5}$ ft 12 110 $6^6 6^7 5^8 5^6$

By comparing the earlier illustration with this one, it becomes evident that we have permitted Horsey Horsey to get closer and closer on the pace until, in his last time out, he falls short of winning the race by a single length. But is his ability to stay on the pace really improved? Hardly, for we also changed the times of the races. We have made his last race, the October 10th event in which he was so close on the pace, the slowest in time of the three races. So there is the illusion of Horsey Horsey's improved ability to stay on the pace, but what has really occurred is that in his last race he was pitted against lowergrade competition than he had in his previous races, and resultantly the pace of this race was substantially slower. Indeed, he himself ran a better race on October 5th when his time was 1:48$\frac{1}{2}$ than on October 10th when his time was 1:49$\frac{1}{5}$.

Pace is tricky, admittedly. But it's manageable. And, now and again—not always, to be sure—but now and again, you'll find that, if handled intelligently, it will reward you munificently.

Onward now, to Class.

CHAPTER 8

Class Will Tell

CLASS IS THE CARDINAL FACTOR of handicapping. Find the horse with the highest class and you've traveled to the end of the rainbow where, as every horse player's children know, there's a pot of pari-mutuel win tickets. But it's one thing to say that the horse with the highest class usually wins and another thing to find that horse. So it is that, prior to any discussion of handicapping techniques for the determination of class, it will be well to define it.

Class has been as variously defined by players as truth has been by poets. And just as the high, smooth brows of poets have yet to reach agreement on What Is Truth, so have the lower, sweaty brows of handicappers failed of agreement on What Is Class.

For instance, the class of a horse has been defined as his value on the market. The speediest horse has been put forth as the classiest horse. Class has been offered as a synonym for personality, making the horse with the highest type of personality the class horse in the race. The pragmatic insist that the horse with the highest earnings is *ipso facto* the horse with the highest class. Consistency, many assert, is the steadiest pointer to a horse's class. Class is "heart," others say. Class is a combination of a horse's ability to stay on the pace and his final time, still others maintain. Inherent racing ability is a not uncommon definition for class. Breeding is the key to class, say some. Class has been held out as the ability to run and win route distances, or the ability to run well carrying heavy weight, or as a quality belonging to the horse that carries the greatest weight over any distance in the shortest time.

While all of these definitions have a reasonable claim to being the true key to class, I lean to the last one, to wit, that the class horse in any race is that horse who has demonstrated his ability to carry the heaviest weight over any distance in the shortest time. Or, to paraphrase General Nathan Bedford Forrest, the horse that gets thar fustest with the mostest is *the* class horse. My footnote for this definition is that the horse must also have proven himself capable of doing so regardless of the pace that was set.

A word now about class and personality, then a charming true story about class and breeding, and then we'll adjust our green eye shade, light up, and get to the techniques of handicapping the class factor.

In the paragraph listing definitions of class we noted personality. There are people who talk a blue streak in their family settings, or amongst their close friends, but place them amongst people whom they sense are their betters and these life-of-the-partyers become as retiring as a morning glory at dusk. It's the same with some horses. Sometimes a horse who has won a race against other horses in crack time will lose another race, notwithstanding the substantially slower time of the losing race as compared to his winning effort. And pace will have nothing to do with it! It's simply that horses, like people, will sometimes sense that they are in company that is in some vague, indefinable way, superior to them. And so they hang back, almost deferentially, and in losing justify their sense of inferiority.

I promised you a true story on breeding and class. It is an axiom of thoroughbred breeding that class is transmitted through hereditary lines. The Cinderellas of the turf are largely confined to the movies. In real life, racing champions are usually princes and princesses, the offspring of thoroughbred royalty. In this connection, it was the view of Italy's late Senator Federico Tesio, one of racing's all-time great breeders and trainers, that even the circumstances in which a horse was conceived played an important role in determining the class of the animal. In a discussion of artificial insemination, Tesio conceded that a horse conceived in this manner was physically indistinguishable from one conceived as a result of nature's ways.

But he pointed out that for some twenty years not a single classic or semiclassic race had been won anywhere in the world by a horse conceived through artificial insemination! Tesio's point was that in the act of intercourse there is transmitted through genes a nervous energy, a kind of vitality, which reposes in the embryo and which comes to fruition in the grown horse in the form of "drive" or "heart." This "heart" is the factor that determines which of two evenly matched horses locked in a grueling stretch duel will display the tenacity and courage necessary to win. In short, this nervous energy, generated by and transmitted in intercourse, contributes to the class that tells.

With this introduction to the importance of the manner in which a thoroughbred is conceived, we are ready for Tesio's story. The story appeared in *Breeding the Racehorse*, by Federico Tesio, published in London by J. A. Allen and Co. It was translated from the original Italian by Edward Spinola. Here 'tis.

"In 1880 or thereabouts a Neapolitan gentleman, Cavaliere Ginistrelli, moved his thoroughbred breeding stock from Portici, near Naples, to Newmarket, with the intention of defeating the English on their own ground.

"Cavaliere Ginistrelli was a 'character' with original ideas. He immediately achieved a clamorous success by breeding a beautiful filly who was given the name of Signorina and who became a top star in her field. In 1892 Signorina, by then a five-year-old, was retired as a broodmare.

"In the meantime the busy little Neapolitan had built himself a house in Newmarket in which his bedroom adjoined the loose-box of his favourite. A window near the head of his bed enabled him to keep an eye on her at any hour of the day or night.

"In spite of these attentions the beautiful Signorina was beginning to grow old without having given birth to a single colt of real quality, although bred to the most famous sires of her day.

"In the spring of 1904 Cavaliere Ginistrelli had arranged to wed Signorina to the great Isinglass, whose services were in high demand at a fee of 300 guineas to be paid at the time of betrothal.

"Both the stallion and his bride-to-be were living in the town of Newmarket, at opposite ends of a long, wide street called—I need hardly say—the High Street. During the breeding season it was the custom to promenade the third class stallions, victims of unemployment, up and down this thoroughfare with their names in large letters seductively embroidered on their blankets.

"On a certain morning in April the comely Signorina was on her way down the High Street to become the bride of the renowned Isinglass. She was led by a stable boy and followed on foot by Cavaliere Ginistrelli, who never let her out of sight on these occasions. Thus she met coming toward her one of those humble thoroughbred stallions with his name, 'Chaleureux,' on his blanket.

"Chaleureux proved worthy of the name. Stopping to savour Signorina's scent, he at once gave signs of a violent infatuation and refused to move another step. Signorina looked upon him with equal favour and also refused to move on. No amount of tugging or pleading had any effect and an amused crowd began to gather.

"But Ginistrelli who was a psychologist as well as a biologist, sized up the situation at a glance.

" 'They love!' he exclaimed. 'A love match it shall be.'

"And so the proud Isinglass pocketed the 300 guineas, but waited in vain for his assignation with the fair Signorina.

"Eleven months later Signorina gave birth to a filly who was given the name of Signorinetta.

"The experts, convinced that Ginistrelli was out of his mind, were openly scornful of Chaleureux's love-child. But Signorinetta grew up to be one of the greatest fillies of all time, winning the Derby and—two days later—the Oaks, a double feat which only two fillies since 1780 had been able to accomplish.

"These facts are true and I was personally acquainted with all five of the individuals involved: Ginistrelli, Isinglass, Chaleureux, Signorina, and Signorinetta."

Tesio, a highly regarded biologist as well as horseman,

whose experiments in horse-breeding were refinements of
Father Mendel's work with peas, concludes his point
about the circumstances of conception and class by
telling us that a subsequent, *pre-arranged* date between
Signorinetta and Chaleureux produced another beautiful
filly. She raced until she was five years old and never
won once!

Nice story?

Now to the determination of class. When we discussed
types of races we found that we had but to look in the
racing program or in the *Daily Racing Form*, or ask the
guy next to us, the one with the ridiculous tie, and we'd
learn that this race is a stakes, or claiming, or possibly
a handicap or an allowance race. Weight, age, sex, consistency, and earnings we have seen are also factors
available for the simple effort of reading. We have
learned, too, that speed and pace, while not as plainly
apparent as the other factors, are readily assessed by
anyone who received as high a grade as C-minus in his
junior high school math course. But class, it's different.
Not appreciably more difficult, but different.

In claiming races, class is more readily established than
in stakes, handicap, and allowance races. This is so because we are guided by the price tag placed on the horse
by its connections. For an easy instance, we know that a
horse that has a $10,000 claiming price on it is a higher-
grade animal than one that has been in $3,500 races.

And while this is true, the player must nonetheless
exercise caution in establishing a claiming horse's class.
*To be a $10,000 or an $8,000 or a $2,000 class horse, the
horse should have won, or damn near won, a $10,000 or
$8,000 or what-have-you race.* Running far off the pace
in a $10,000 claiming race, no matter how many such
races the past performances indicate the horse has been
entered in, does not establish that horse as being of a
$10,000 class. No trainer who knows or values his oats
considers it as such, and the horse-player who values
his own oats, the green negotiable variety, shouldn't
either. By the same token, it's safe to assume that there
aren't any horses in a $10,000 (or any other claiming

level) race, who are of a substantially higher class. The reason, we will recall, is that an owner will not enter a patently superior horse in a cheaper claiming event lest he lose him for a song. It is a helpful-to-the-bettor fact of racing that in claiming races the laws of economics work in his behalf insofar as his quest for class is concerned.

When you find a horse that has kept on the pace in a $10,000 claiming race, increase the consideration you give him in proportion to his drop in class. That is, if the horse has stayed on the pace in a $10,000 claiming event, like him in a $9,000 race, like him even more in an $8,500 race, and shower him with affection as the claiming price of the race gets lower.

But be watchful of the reverse situation, where a horse who has run well in a cheaper event has been entered with higher grade animals. Note the following illustration of the past performance records of two horses who are competing today in a $7,000 claiming race:

Horse A:	$5^5 4^2 1^h 1^2$	Jockey^7	6000
	$7^4 5^4 3^3 3^4$	Jockey^3	6500
Horse B:	$3^3 2^4 2^3 2^2$	Jockey^2	7000
	$6^5 6^6 2^4 2^3$	Jockey^8	7500

At first glance, Horse A seems appealing. The race before his last, he remained on the pace from start to finish. His last time out, he won by a full two lengths. Horse A certainly seems to be in condition. Horse B boasts no win in the past performances shown. Indeed, his last race, in which he was two lengths behind the winner, hardly represents a dramatic improvement over his earlier race, though some improvement there is.

Which horse, A or B, is the better bet today?

B, hands down. B gets our nod because today's is a $7,000 claiming race and he has closed on the pace in a $7,500 race. He has run even closer in his last effort, a $7,000 event. Horse A did, of course, win his last outing. However, it was a $6,000 claiming race, and an improvement over a $6,500 event. In short, A improved when he was *dropping* in class, that is, below the class of today's

race. Today's race is for *higher* class animals. B it is who
is staying in his own class. To boot, B too shows improvement and, while not as much as A, B's improvement has
been against higher-class competition. *Ergo* B, $2.00 on
the nose.

The moral of this illustration is that we must not permit
ourselves to get all jazzed up by sparkling past performances, unless the horse sparkled in company whose class
is the same or better than the class the horse is with today.
As with the fighter who has outpointed all of the light-
weights in his division, and is as ready as ever he'll be,
you still aren't going to place your hard-earned do-re-mi
on him if he's entering the ring with a heavyweight, even
an ordinary heavyweight.

One of the special situations in which the player might
bet on a horse who is stepping up in class and not warrant
having his head examined is in the case of a lightly run,
but impressive three-year-old. In this type of situation,
the horse's class may not yet have been established, and
having won the few races in which he's been entered, his
connections keep stepping him up in class. One reason
for this is to avoid his being claimed; the other is simply
to find the appropriate class level in which the animal
belongs.

As a general rule, however—indeed as one of racing's
firmest rules—horses stepping up in class are not recommended for fans who enjoy winning. Contrariwise, horses
stepping down in class are good bets. My records reveal
that the overwhelming number of claiming races are won
by the stepping down horses.

Movement up and down in class is more meaningful to
the player in the cheaper claiming races than in the more
expensive ones. A drop of $1,000, or a rise, for that
matter, of $1,000, is far more significant with horses in
$4,000 claiming events than it is with their uptown rela-
tions in $18,000 events.

Often, claiming races feature horses whose past performances reveal Alw or HcpO races. (Didn't forget those
abbreviations, already, did you? Look 'em up. I'm not
repeating their meaning.) In such cases we are without

our claiming tags to guide us to the horse's class. In these situations it is important to bear in mind that, like the man who wears pants but isn't panting, the horse who's been in an allowance or handicap race isn't necessarily an allowance or handicap class horse. The thing to look for is, Did the horse stay on the pace of those races, or better still, did it win? If it did, it's a class horse and a good bet to handle claiming platers. If it did not, it cannot be assumed that the horse is of a higher class than its claiming confreres in today's race. The horse may have been doing well as a claiming horse and, in order to avoid its being claimed, it's connections placed him in an allowance race. In this way the animal is kept sharp while its trainer is waiting for a right spot for it in another claiming race.

In judging the class of horses in allowance, handicap, and stakes races, we fly solo. No claiming prices here to guide, accelerate, or brake our handicapper's enthusiasm. We are instead called upon to apply the savvy that we have accumulated in this book. Fortunately, the information we require and upon which we are called upon to lavish our learning is available in the *Daily Racing Form*.

The following are the personality and behavioral traits an understanding of which enables us to establish the horse with the class that will tell, in allowance, handicap, and stakes races.

Does the horse's past performance record reveal consistent, as distinguished from erratic, winning efforts?

Even in his losing races, did he usually stay on the pace?

Is the total of his purse money relatively high compared to that of the other horses in the race?

Does he regularly run in classy races?

Does he hold up when assigned heavy weight?

Has he been running at the major tracks? (Remember, a horse who has been running in allowance and in high-priced claiming events at Belmont, Santa Anita, Aqueduct, Hialeah, and the other major tracks cannot be assumed to be of a lower class than a stakes horse who's been balling it up at the minor tracks.)

The horse with the greatest number of Yes answers to these questions will usually be the horse with the telling class.

A final word now, on class. Like last year's twenty-game winner in baseball who this year huffs and puffs while barely eking out eight wins for the season, the class of horses is subject to change. As we have cautioned in our discussions of consistency, speed, and pace, so we caution here: Study the horse's *current* performances, for it's his current class that is meaningful to you and to the state of your current bank account.

CHAPTER 9

Handicapping Systems

As LONG AS MAN EXPERIENCES imperfect health, so long will there be magic potions guaranteed to return youth, vigor, and hair. And regardless of the fact that the fancy and expensive pill is plain aspirin, there will be those who will swear by it. For testimonial writer Mr. L. W. of Dubuque, Iowa the quack potion worked, and you'd be an A Number One jerk to argue science with a curly-haired guy who tells you, "They used to call me baldy, until . . ."

All of which is by way of introducing the subject of this chapter: "Handicapping Systems." As long as there are horse-players there will be systems that purport to be *the* panacea for losing bettors. I, the sane, steady voice of science, am here to tell you that the concept of a winning system is pure meadow bull pie. Still, having no reason to be skeptical of Mr. L. W. of Dubuque or wherever the hell he's from, and having even less reason to doubt some of my track friends, I do concede that for some players, some systems do work . . . I suppose.

Prior to relating some of the handicapping systems that

are most frequently employed, let's take a look at the Achilles' heel with which all handicapping systems are afflicted. It will be useful in terms of encouraging the reader to use systems discriminately. It may even protect the reader against quack systems the purveyors of which are in constant search of the Mr. L. W.'s of grandstand society.

The very word *system*, with its implication of a formula for selecting winners, defeats itself. There can be no formula for *systematically* predicting honest horse races. Indeed, were horse-racing results conducive to systematized prediction, the IBM people would long since have devised a Univac to get at it and do it. Also, we can reasonably assume that were the sundry systems hawked in turf publications and at tracks, really endowed with the magic powers claimed for them by their proponents, said proponents would not be pleading with you, you total stranger you, to buy their Midas systems for a lousy fifty cents. *N'est-ce pas?*

Systems are like stereotypes. Englishmen, for instance, are said to have a wry sense of humor. Then again, Jack the Ripper was an Englishman. Because each race, like Englishmen and girls, is different, each one must be individually appraised. The system is a *general* formula without capacity to provide for the innumerable variations presented by each race.

In this book we have considered such ponderables as the types of races, weight, sex, age, consistency, speed, pace, and class. However, what of such imponderables as the current physical and mental disposition of the horse, the same of the jockey, the intentions of the trainer, the effect of the horse's preceding night's sleep and of his breakfast, the jockey's same, the circumstances of the race itself, with its unforeseeable traffic jams, blocks, openings, and bumps? And even if half of these variables were capable of being anticipated by a system, how would the system provide for that elusive but omnipresent factor called racing luck? No, Virginia, there is no system.

Another weakness common to most systems is the very

fact that some races defy even the rational processes of handicapping. Defying the logic of handicapping, such races couldn't very well be subject to forecasting through a blanket kind of system. In this category of races that are beyond logical handicapping are some cheap claiming events, the contestants in which are so erratic that your grandmother's intuition has little less chance of success than your handicapping know-how. Nor are very cheap events the only races that are best left alone. Any race, be it stakes, handicap, allowance, or claiming, may turn up three, possibly four, substantially evenly matched favorites. Under these circumstances the bettor would do well to pass the race by. Not only is this kind of race too difficult to handicap, but come pay-off time the return will hardly compensate for the risk involved. And Audax, the late, great British turf authority, once opined that it was his golden rule for bettors that they *never* wager the result of a handicap race. His reasoning? That the racing secretary has deliberately, and with malice aforethought, assigned weight handicaps for the purpose of equalizing the winning chances of all the horses. Why then, in placing a bat on Stubby Legs, should you bet against all of the other evenly matched horses in the race *and* against the racing secretary's savvy? Audax believed that weight for age events presented the player with racing's most stable investment opportunities. Smart man, Audax.

Probably the most elementary of handicapping systems employed by racing's laity is to select the winning choice of their favorite public handicapper. And indeed, the handicappers for the major newspapers, for the wire services, and the *Daily Racing Form*, are, by and large, experts in their craft. Their batting averages, however, suffer from the public's requirement that they predict the results of each and every race on the track's program. Because a goodly number of races per day are beyond rational handicapping techniques, even these experts make a sorry over-all showing for almost every racing meeting.

Look at the ensuing charts. The first one reveals what would have been the profit-and-loss net to two-dollar players who employed the handicapping system of betting their favorite public handicapper's selections for each race during recent meetings at Aqueduct, Belmont, and Saratoga. I have substituted for the actual name of the expert the letters A, B, C, etc. In so doing, I am protecting the innocent, because these men are, in fact, expert handicappers. Their poor showing, however, is the result of their having to predict the results of so many unpredictable races. The second chart describes the profit and loss net under the same circumstances for the meetings at Garden State, Monmouth, and Atlantic City.

AQUEDUCT, BELMONT, SARATOGA

Handicapper	Number of Selections	Profit	Loss
A	1178		178.80
B	1186		232.30
C	1187		256.80
D	1188		289.00
E	1186		293.80
F	1178		296.00
G	1188		348.30
H	1187		392.90
I	1185		442.00
J	1177		518.60
K	1188		522.50

GARDEN STATE, MONMOUTH, ATLANTIC CITY

Handicapper	Number of Selections	Profit	Loss
I	714		138.20
G	716		236.60
H	714		244.60
C	715		269.30
J	705		313.40
K	713		313.60
F	706		324.00
A	707		351.20
E	715		410.80
D	715		439.60
B	714		447.80

These charts are by no means unrepresentative. With costly eloquence they testify to the futility of betting every race, even when doing so on the recommendations of the experts.

Still, systems do serve a constructive purpose. Those that are in common usage thrive on more than simply the hope that springs eternal in all gamblers. To persist, they must have proven helpful to some players some of the time. It being in the nature of the gambler to recall his winnings and to block out on his losings, he remembers well, and talks about, the methods by which he has won. And so a system lives on, tantalizing gamblers with the fantasy of the big kill. In addition to this somewhat dubious value, systems have the very real value of controlling and limiting the player's losings. The reason for this is that by and large there *is* some reason to a system's rhyme. Consequently, system-playing is at least superior to the haphazard guess work that passes for handicapping on the part of so many of the folks who drop by the seller's window.

Now for the systems.

Betting horses that have been claimed their last time out. This system takes the word of the owner or trainer who has claimed the horse, and in doing so has expressed his educated view that the horse is a winner. Else, the cost of hay being what it is, why should he have claimed it? A desirable built-in feature of this system is the racing rule that, once a horse is claimed, he must be entered in his next race at a higher claiming price than the race from which he was claimed. The betting public, noting the higher claiming price for this race, assumes that the horse is competing against high-class thoroughbreds and proceeds to ignore the horse, thereby raising his odds and, when the system works, the pay-off price, as well. Many bettors who are partial to this system (I like it, too) will stay with the horse in its second outing even if it didn't win in its first effort under its new colors. This continued confidence in the animal is rooted in the hope that, now that the horse has returned to its own claiming range, it will show the mettle that prompted the new owner to claim it.

Betting the horse with the biggest drop in class. This system, another one with which the player may enjoy spurts of success, can be employed in two ways. Some there are who will bet the horse with the biggest drop in class since his last race. Others prefer the variation that sees them bet the horse with the biggest drop in class from the highest class at which the horse has won. I deem the latter twin in this system to be the Toni; the former, the phoney. A horse's true class can only be determined by the competition over which he prevailed, not the competition with which he "also ran." Consequently, a drop in class for a horse that has not won in the higher class company it used to keep is not necessarily a true drop in class. The horse's connections, in dropping the horse, may simply be trying to determine the horse's true class. However, when we note the horse with the biggest drop in class from the highest class in which it has won, we are dealing with an actual drop in actual class.

Betting the top weighted horse. This system is pragmatic. It is based on the fact that the top weighted horse is so burdened because the track secretary deems it to be the best of the lot, or because its past performances so establish it, and consequently, under the conditions of the race, it is top weighted. This system is a good show bet, but because of the small return it yields on two dollars, it's best for big bettors.

Betting the horse with the highest earnings. The idea behind this system is a variation on the old saw, If You're So Smart, Why Aren't You Rich? It assumes that the horse that is so rich is pretty smart in his racing ways. Some will consider the horses' total earnings and choose the one with the highest figure. Some will concern themselves only with the horses' earnings at the current meeting. Still others will bet the horse with the highest average earnings over its last few races, or the horse with the highest average earnings within a given length of time preceding the date of the race.

Betting the horse with the highest speed rating. If you are going to use speed ratings as a system after all that I have said in my chapters on speed and pace, go ahead, but remember that I told you so. You *are* going to use it? Well then, use speed ratings for sprint races only. It is well, too, to restrict the system to speed ratings earned during the past month, at the same track at which the horse is now running, and for the same distance that it is being called upon to race today.

Betting the favorite in races with no more than three, or four at the most, horses with less than 10 to 1 odds. The idea behind this system is that notwithstanding that there may be eight, nine, ten, or more horses competing, there are but three or four horses who have more than a prayer of a chance to strut 'round the winner's circle. I recommend it as a system for big-time show bettors.

Betting on stables. Those partial to this system reason that the wealthiest stables can afford the best yearlings and can provide these yearlings with the finest of conditioning facilities. The practitioners of this system assume that if a successful stable deems a horse worthy of racing under its colors, then that horse is likely to be a winner.

Betting the trainer. This one is like predicting a pennant winner in baseball, on the basis of comparing the talents of the managers rather than of the teams. The horse-racing page of the sports section of some dailies, turf publications, and the racing programs of many tracks cite the leading trainers for the various meetings. A leading trainer is simply one who has sent more horses to the post who have returned winners than have his confreres.

Betting the jockey. People who bet the jockey, regardless of the identity of his mount, are so numerous that they frequently affect the odds. A Cauthen or a Shoemaker may have the mount on a horse that should go off at 12 to 1. Immediately, however, that the public reads the name of the famous rider, it reacts with a rush of confidence powered by enough two-dollar bets to depress the odds. And often the odds will fall below a sensible price for the horse who, rather than the jockey, is really going to do the running. Still, this is a popular system, and not without reason. Just as Hollywood's brightest stars have first call on that colony's most desirable movie parts, turfdom's top-rated riders get the prime selection of mounts. After a jockey has proven his exceptional talent, the owners of superior horses seek him out—as an insurance for their anticipated wins. So it is that, notwithstanding the fact that the world's ablest rider can't make a stakes horse out of a plater, top jockeys are nonetheless fairly good bets. Many a player is here to say that by betting this or that leading jockey he has emerged from a meeting in the black.

Betting the consensus. Racing's publications and the daily newspaper carry a number of syndicated as well as staff public handicappers. The consensus selection is that horse who is the choice of most of these handicappers. The consensus selection is a system of handicapping used by dilettantes and by the kind of guy who gets kicks from frequent trips to the cashier's window, notwithstanding the fact that his wallet may be lighter at the end of the ninth race than it was before the first race.

My point is that consensus selections do win frequently, sometimes as much as 50 percent of the time; but, and it's a big but, the pay-off on these heavy favorites is so low that the consensus player, over an extended period, is a sure loser.

Betting on the basis of consistency. In our chapter on consistency, rather imaginatively titled "It's Not the Hobgoblin of Little Minds," we discussed a variety of handicapping systems that bear rereading at this point. The chapter began on page 28. I'll wait for you to reread it.

Ready, now, to continue? In an additional variation on consistency systems the practitioner rates a horse's last five races with five points for each win, three points for each time the horse placed, and one point for each show position. The horse with the highest total is the selection. Some consistency players employ this one by rating the horse's performances during the course of the past month or two rather than using an arbitrary five races, which may include old indexes.

Overlay system. An overlay exists when the morning line posts probable odds for a horse who actually goes off at considerably higher odds. By illustration, a public handicapper may estimate Twinkle Toes as going off at 3 to 1. At post time, the public sends Twinkle Toes off at 9 to 1. The overlay system bettor runs, does not walk, to the nearest seller's window and asserts his support for Twinkle Toes' number. Why? He reasons that the handicapper knows something about TT that the public doesn't.

Underlay system. In this system of handicapping, the circumstances are reversed, but the system player still runs, does not walk, you know where. Underlays occur when the morning line or a public handicapper estimates Peg Leg to go off at, say, 10 to 1. However, when the loudspeaker blares, "They're at the post!" the tote board reveals that Peg Leg is at 4 or 3, or such, to 1. In this situation the underlay system player assumes that word has gotten out that Peg Leg is going to do it today. Else, the player reasons, how come his odds have fallen way down?

There are more, many more, systems. They range from picking horses with cute names through picking certain post positions, on up to complicated arithmetical formulas in which weight, distance, speed ratings, and what all are assigned plus and minus numbers and the system player makes like Albert Einstein. Having had my say on the use of systems earlier in this chapter, I will not again impose on the gentle reader my lack of enthusiasm for this type of handicapping—except to make this final observation.

Handicapping systems ain't fun. The fun of handicapping the races is in tackling each race on its own terms. There's the challenge! Systems? It's like a doctor who prescribes aspirin for every set of symptoms. It works often enough, but for this he had to go to medical school? And if you plan to use systems, dope, why'd you read the other chapters?

CHAPTER 10

Betting Systems

THE METHODOLOGY OF INVESTMENT PROCEDURES, herein indelicately referred to as betting systems, can determine whether at the racing day's end you will strut home with the jaunty smugness of a winner or whether, a loser, you will afix a brave, toothy, but let's face it, false smile, as a mask for your dog-eared, guilt-ridden face.

Intelligent betting methods can compensate for the losses resulting from imperfect handicapping. Unintelligent betting methods can foul up fairly good handicapping. Many is the time that I have seen a player who has cashed three tickets all day wind up with more of the pari-mutuel's goodies than another player who selected the same horses plus two or three others whose tickets were negotiable. And the first guy, he of the wise betting methods, did not place larger bets than the second guy, he of the sharp selections but dull investments!

In this chapter we will discuss a number of betting systems, and here and there, as a public service, I will reach into my rich-but-not-all-roses experience for the purpose of cautioning, guiding, and enlightening the unwary investor.

The oldest and still the most common wagering system is the one known in ancient Pompeii as *Bettingus Haphazardus*. In *Bettingus Haphazardus* early afternoon winners, with what may pass for Christian charity or may well be just plain damn foolishness, pour their loot back into the pari-mutuel's jaws during the later afternoon, like they had something awful against coming out ahead. A variation of the *B. H.* system sees early losers, in their attempts to bail themselves out, fall deeper and deeper into the quicksand of their losses. As a matter of professional pride and out of deference to the sophistication of my reading public, I do not deign to discuss *Bettingus Haphazardus*.

Next to *B. H.* (it does *not* mean Before Hialeah), the most common system of wagering is flat betting. This one merits our consideration.

In flat betting the same amount of money is bet on each bettable race. That is, the player may bet two dollars on his first selection and, regardless of the result, he will bet two dollars on his next selection, and so on for the rest of the afternoon.

Inasmuch as some 30 per cent of the favorites win, it might appear to some that flat betting the favorites to win is a valid betting system. Not so. The fact is that the average pay-off on winning favorites is under six dollars. The arithmetic of collecting under six dollars for one out of three two-dollar bets indicates that flat betting favorites to win is a losing proposition. In races where the favorites go off at even money or less, about 50 per cent of the favorites win. Again the return is so small as to suggest that flat betting these favorites to win is, if not an actual losing proposition, still a long way from the road to Easy Street.

In this regard, flat betting does have an advantage over most other systems. It controls and limits your losses. Even in the unlikely event that each of your selections for the day runs in total disregard of your confidence in it, the cost of your afternoon's entertainment has been little more than an evening at the theatre. And then, no small amount of the theatre you've seen lately was also presented with little regard for you.

To be successful, flat betting on the nose requires a handicapping know-how that exceeds the 30 per cent wins of favorites, or failing this, includes in its 30 per cent a horse or horses that pay more than a two-to-one price. More frequent trips can be made to the cashier's window by flat betting the place position, and still more frequent visits to the cashier will result from flat betting the show position. This increased socializing with the cashier, however, does not mean that a greater financial return will be realized than through win betting. The fact is that the greater percentage of favorites that place, compared to those that win, and the still greater percentage that show, compared to place and win, do not compensate for the sharp decrease in money returned for these positions.

In other words, let us assume that Tom flat bets the favorite to win in stakes races. Ricardo flat bets the favorites to place, and Herschel flat bets the favorites to show. In stakes races, over a period of time, Tom will cash 40 per cent of his tickets, Ricardo will cash 60 per cent of his tickets, and Herschel might cash as many as 80 per cent of his tickets. Notwithstanding Herschel's hustling and bustling between his seat and the pay-off window, at the end of the experiment he will have not done as well as Ricardo. And Tom, our all-American hero, will have stashed away the most moolah, notwithstanding his having cashed the least number of tickets. It's all the result of the ratio of pay-off prices between win and place and show.

To illustrate this very important lesson, I have tabulated the race results of a randomly selected day at four different tracks. In each program, at Belmont, at Atlantic City, at Lincoln Downs, and at Hawthorne, we have flat bet the favorites to win, to place, and to show. The results follow:

PAY-OFF PRICES ON FLAT BETTING THE FAVORITES

Belmont	Win	Place	Show
1st race	5.50	3.30	2.90
2d race	x	x	3.20
3d race	5.30	3.10	2.40
4th race	4.50	2.60	2.50
5th race	x	x	x
6th race	4.90	3.20	2.70
7th race	x	x	2.90
8th race	x	x	x
9th race	x	x	x

PAY-OFF PRICES ON FLAT BETTING THE FAVORITES
(*Continued*)

Atlantic City

1st race	x	x	x
2d race	3.60	3.00	2.40
3d race	5.20	4.20	3.40
4th race	4.00	3.20	2.60
5th race	x	x	x
6th race	5.40	3.60	3.20
7th race	x	3.60	2.80
8th race	x	x	2.40

Lincoln Downs

1st race	x	3.40	2.80
2d race	4.40	3.20	2.60
3d race	5.00	2.80	2.40
4th race	x	x	x
5th race	x	3.80	3.00
6th race	x	x	x
7th race	x	3.20	2.20
8th race	x	x	x
9th race	x	x	x

Hawthorne

1st race	5.20	3.80	3.00
2d race	x	x	x
3d race	x	3.60	2.40
4th race	x	x	x
5th race	7.80	4.20	3.00
6th race	x	x	2.60
7th race	7.60	4.20	3.00
8th race	x	3.40	2.80
9th race	x	x	x

$2 *Flat Bet Return,*	*Win*	*Place*	*Show*
Net:	—1.60	—4.60	—6.80

The chart graphically testifies to a number of truths to which we have paid homage in these pages. To wit:

Favorites ain't money-makers.

Still, flat betting favorites, be it for win, place, or show, is cheaper than going to the theatre.

Show players get more exercise than place players as they traffic between their seats and the cashier, and place players, in turn, wear their shoes out sooner than win players.

In order to come out in the black, win players who flat bet favorites and consequently win some 30 per cent of the time, must snag at least one winner that pays better than two to one.

Of course, the player who handicaps the races without regard to favorites-shmavorites, and does his homework so that I will be proud of him, will find the flat betting system profitable.

Uptown cousin of the flat betting system is the system of Betting Across the Board. In this system of wagering, the player bets an equal amount of money on Hobby Horse to win, to place, and to show. For instance, a two-dollar bet across-the-board means a six-dollar investment, two singletons of which say the horse will win, another two bucks say it's going to place, and the remaining two bills say that Hobby Horse will show. The place bet is intended to hedge the win bet, and the show bet to hedge the place bet. Five dollars across the board involves a fifteen-dollar investment, and so on.

In my comments on flat betting we have seen that flat betting the favorite to either win, place, or show will result at best in inconsequential winnings, and at worst, in modest losses. Certainly, if flat betting favorites as a system on the win or place or show position is a losing system, then across-the-board betting of favorites is trebly bad—for the player, not, to be sure, for the track or the state.

The knowledgeable handicapper will apply his savvy to each race on its own merits, and if his is the courage of his convictions he will do better by investing the entire six dollars on the nose of his selection. If he's a good handicapper he'll come out further ahead as a result of the proportionately higher win prices, and if he's the kind of handicapper that requires additional seasoning, he'll have the satisfaction of having lost less than he would have by betting across the board.

The one exception to this advice is when your handicapping has you come up with a horse that is going off at a long-shot price of ten to one or more. In these single shot situations the place and show prices are usually going to be substantially higher than in the case of low-priced favorites. Across-the-board betting under these circumstances provides not only a sense of security, but a meaningful hedge in the event that the horse doesn't quite live up to your expectations.

We have seen that there is a kind of geometrical regression of pay-off prices from win to place and from place to show. A system of betting that may be termed the Geometrical Progression System has been devised to offset this regression. A variation of across-the-board betting, this system sees the player bet X dollars on Soaring Hopes to win, two times X dollars on Soaring Hopes to place, and anywhere from four to six times X dollars on Soaring Hopes to show. The idea is that if the horse, failing to win, places, the place and show money will still give the player a profit. Further, if the horse, failing either to win or place, shows, the large amount of money bet on the show position will make up the losses on the win and place position, and maybe even provide a small profit. Quite plainly, if the horse wins, the geometrical progression player is in clover. No less plainly, if the horse runs out of the money, the player is in bitter herbs.

As in the case of flat betting and across-the-board betting, the geometrical progression system works well enough for better than average handicappers. Applied to favorites, it works well on those days when the favorites work well—for instance, in Atlantic City, in the Geometrical Progression Chart, when four of eight favorites romped home as winners. But comes a day when the favorites received their come-uppance from rank outsiders, as in the Lincoln Downs section of the Geometrical Progression Chart. Now, you're in trouble—geometrically progressive trouble. In the Belmont section of the chart, note that, notwithstanding the fact that four favorites won, the system failed. Why? Because three favorites ran completely out of the money.

Where a geometrical progression system is employed on favorites, and the fan bets two dollars to win, four dollars to place, and twelve dollars to show, it is necessary for at least 75 per cent of the favorites to run in the money, and for some three, at least, to actually win in order for the system to ring up a profit. In view of this, geometrical progression betting on favorites is best reserved for stakes races. Of course, where a player is exercising his own handicapping insights, indifferent to which horse the general public is knighting as favorite, the geometrical progression way of betting will geometrically increase his winnings—if he's a good handicapper. Finally, as a system, note that the geometrical progression chart and the flat betting chart cover the identical races. The flat bettors, on the whole, did better. They usually do.

PAY-OFF PRICES ON GEOMETRICAL PROGRESSION
BETTING
$2 to Win, $4 to Place, $12 to Show

Belmont	Win	Place	Show	Profit (+) Loss (−)
1st race	5.50	3.30	2.90	+11.50
2d race	x	x	3.20	+ 1.20
3d race	5.30	3.10	2.40	+ 7.90
4th race	4.50	2.60	2.50	+ 6.70
5th race	x	x	x	−18.00
6th race	4.90	3.20	2.70	+ 9.50
7th race	x	x	2.90	− .60
8th race	x	x	x	−18.00
9th race	x	x	x	−18.00
				−17.80 net
Atlantic City				
1st race	x	x	x	−18.00
2d race	3.60	3.00	2.40	+ 6.00
3d race	5.20	4.20	3.40	+16.00
4th race	4.00	3.20	2.60	+ 8.00
5th race	x	x	x	−18.00

PAY-OFF PRICES ON GEOMETRICAL PROGRESSION
BETTING (*Continued*)

6th race	5.40	3.60	3.20	+13.80
7th race	x	3.60	2.80	+ 6.00
8th race	x	x	2.40	− 3.60
				+10.20 net

Lincoln Downs

1st race	x	3.40	2.80	+ 5.60
2d race	4.40	3.20	2.60	+ 8.40
3d race	5.00	2.80	2.40	+ 7.00
4th race	x	x	x	−18.00
5th race	x	3.80	3.00	+ 7.60
6th race	x	x	x	−18.00
7th race	x	3.20	2.20	+ 1.60
8th race	x	x	x	−18.00
9th race	x	x	x	−18.00
				−41.80 net

Hawthorne

1st race	5.20	3.80	3.00	+12.80
2d race	x	x	x	−18.00
3d race	x	3.60	2.40	+ 3.60
4th race	x	x	x	−18.00
5th race	7.80	4.20	3.00	+16.20
6th race	x	x	2.60	− 2.40
7th race	7.60	4.20	3.00	+16.00
8th race	x	3.40	2.80	+ 5.60
9th race	x	x	x	−18.00
				− 2.20 net
				−51.60 Total Net

Just as across-the-board betting developed as an extension of flat betting, so does the Doubling Up system suggest itself as a development of geometrical progression betting. Doubling up, however, is far more talked about than it is practiced. And understandably so. In this system the player bets, say, ten dollars on the first race. If he loses, he bets twenty dollars on the next race. Should he lose again, he bets forty dollars on the following race. In the event that a doubling-up plunger ran a string of eight losses, as happens to the best of handicappers, the ninth race, at this rate, would require a $2,560 bet!

I make mention of this system on the not unlikely chance that the Aga Khan may have been waiting for my book. I recommend it to you, Aga, buddy, and beg the indulgence of our other readers while I caution you to use this system only in countries where private enterprise bookmaking is legal. For should you use this system at the track, and find it necessary to place a ninth or tenth or (zounds!) eleventh or twelfth string-of-losers bet, the amount of your bet ($21,280 on the twelfth bet) would so depress the odds on your selection as to render your sporting efforts hardly worthwhile. Understand, Aga, buddy? Remember that.

We return now to our own land where, since we are shareholders in our glorious income tax system, Uncle Sam protects us from the frustrations of great wealth such as annoy the Aga Khan. Amongst ourselves again, we continue with betting systems that are of this world.

The Day's Quota System, while requiring some courage and a nest egg bigger than a swallow's, is manageable for many players. In this system the player stipulates to himself how much he wishes to win for the day. Nothing silly, though. That is, an *aficionado* of modest means may realistically set himself a goal of twenty dollars. A better-healed guy may establish his goal for the day as fifty dollars, and so on up the income ladder. Let us illustrate the day's quota system as it would be plied by the humble race trackster who seeks a twenty-dollar net for the afternoon.

In the first bettable race, our player's choice goes off at three to one. The system calls for the bettor to plunk down seven dollars on his selection's nose. If the horse wins, he has won twenty-one dollars, *and he quits for the day*. In short, he's made his goal and he takes to heart the Psalm of Our Lady of Las Vegas, "Quitteth Thou Whilst Thou Art Ahead." If he loses, his goal is twenty dollars plus the seven he lost. Comes the next bettable race. His choice is a horse the chances of which the public has established as one in four. This time the system again requires a seven-dollar investment. (The player's goal is twenty-seven dollars. By betting seven dollars at four to one, the return is twenty-eight dollars, the nearest amount to twenty-seven dollars.) If the horse wins, the player folds his tent. If it loses, his goal is now thirty-four dollars. In the latter event, assuming that his next selection is a two-to-one choice, his bet will have to be seventeen dollars, and so on until he reaches his winning goal, or debtor's goal.

As a matter of demonstrable mathematical fact, as well as of feasibility (the system does require money, but not remotely the kind involved in doubling up), this is the surest and safest system of betting that I know. I urge its users, however, to set manageable goals for themselves.

As distinguished from betting systems, there are two betting gimmicks, as it were, that warrant brief comment. I refer to parlays and daily doubles.

Parlays call for the reinvestment in a second race of winnings earned in a prior race. For instance, a two-horse parlay might see me receive $9.80 for my troubles in the first race. My next bet would have me place the entire $10.00 on my selection. A three-horse parlay involves the same procedure repeated an additional time. The hazard involved in parlay betting is losing. A player who has selected two winners who have paid nice prices loses it all if the third race is disappointing. On the other hand, the parlay's dangerous living has a built-in safety valve. The money you lose is not yours; it's the track's, plus your original investment. The advantage of the parlay is that if you win, man, you win big.

I recommend that parlay players confine themselves to the better-grade races. The inconsistency of cheaper horses militates against using them for parlay betting. The wisdom of this advice is evidenced by the few times one wins the daily double—which invariably includes the cheaper races on the day's card.

In the daily double form of betting, the bettor selects the horses in the first and second race, to win. While the daily double price almost always exceeds the return to be garnered from the parlaying of the first two races, it is not a good investment. My records of several hundred daily doubles stand behind this flat statement. The reasons for the speculativeness of daily doubles are to be found in the kinds of races the program openers usually are: cheap races. Remember, 30 per cent of the favorites of all races win. That figure includes the stakes and handicap races where the winning favorites exceed 30 per cent. The two-plus-two of this fact suggests that the percentage of winning favorites in the cheap races must be less than 30 per cent, in order for the overall average to reach the 30 per cent level. The daily double being made up of the cheaper claiming events, its favorites are amongst the least predictable. A betting gimmick structured around the least consistent horses in the cast is primarily designed for the amusement of the track and the state—not of the bettor.

Still, sporty me bets the daily double all the time, and other forms of multiple wagering, too: the triple, the twin double, the exacta, and the perfecta. Why? Because it's fun, and that, my friends, is what a day at the races is all about: fun. As soon as it becomes a business venture for you, look out, you're really not enjoying it any longer.

CHAPTER 11

Gold Nuggets

THIS CHAPTER CONSISTS OF A COMPENDIUM of helpful handicapping hints. Some are digests of important factors that have been explained more fully in the preceding text. Some are handicapping aids not previously discussed, but requiring no extensive explanations. All are negotiable gold nuggets. Before you leave for the track when next the spirit moves you, reread this chapter, my equine Koran. Do it the next few times you go. It will pay.

Ready, now?

• Don't bet on tips, the "hot" variety, the poop "direct from the stable," the "sure thing" from the jockey's girl of the night before, or "the Word" from the horse's own mouth. If there is any inside information to be had, what you *can* bet on is that it's being guarded like it was the Hope Diamond—so as to keep the odds from falling. Stay with the racing form. In the long run it's cheaper and more reliable.

• Don't buy the green sheets, the blue sheets, the turquoise, and shocking pink sheets. If the good Samaritans who publish them know so much, they'd be betting the horses themselves rather than giving away their winners for the price of a hot dog and coffee.

• Don't bet on every race. You don't invest in every stock issue. Pick your spots, like you do your other investments.

• The cheaper the horse, the less consistent his performance; and the more tenuous your investment.

• Horses going down in claiming price are better bets than those going up in claiming price. However, if a horse is entered in a claiming race that is substantially cheaper than the company it has been keeping, look out. Something may be the matter with it. On the other hand, if a horse who has been running well is entered in a claiming race $500 or $1,000 more expensive than his customary company, and it is a lightly raced colt or filly, consider it.

• A horse claimed his last time out, or the race before his last race, warrants consideration. In selecting this horse you are showing respect for the judgment of the trainer who purchased it, and in purchasing it has said to all and sundry, This horse has It. When a horse is freshly claimed he must be entered at a higher price next time out. This tends to raise his odds—and the pay-off.

• In better-class claiming races at major tracks, beware of the horse whose last outings were allowance races or handicaps at smaller tracks. Don't assume a horse's class because it has a handicap or even stakes race in its past performance. Stakes races in Podunk may be the equivalent of an $8,000 claiming race at Santa Anita.

● Stakes horses excepted, lay off the horse that hasn't been to the post within a month. The cheaper the horse the more recently he needs to have been raced in order to earn your confidence. My records reveal that in claiming races a meaningful number of wins are posted by horses whose last race was within two weeks of their current winning effort.

● Stakes horses excepted, be wary of the horse that has had a nose-to-nose stretch drive his last time out. No matter the heart he may have shown in winning, the effort likely took a lot out of him.

● Stakes horses excepted, ignore a horse that has just been shipped from a distant stable into the track you are visiting. You too need to limber up, rid yourself of kinks, after a long trip.

● All things equal, a horse that has had a race over the track is a better bet than one who has shipped in from another track—even if the other track is in the same county, let alone across the country.

● A sleek-looking horse is usually a healthy horse. If the horse doesn't have that glossy appearance in the paddock, he may not be feeling quite like himself today.

● About 30 per cent of the favorites win. In stakes races, 40 per cent of the favorites win. This does not mean that betting the favorites is a recommended pasttime. The return on the 30 per cent and 40 per cent favorites is so small as to net the player a loss over a period of time. *Ergo*, learn to sort the wheat-favorites from the chaff-favorites.

● If you must be a chalk player, bet the favorite in the ninth race, or if your neighborhood track features only eight races, the eighth race. You'll get higher odds on the favorite in the last race on the card than in any other of the day's events. How come? All the losers, the teaming legions of them, are reaching for the moon, betting the long shots in the foredoomed hope that they'll make it all back in one fell swoop. Consequently, the favorite, ignored by the (m)asses, goes off at a higher price than is warranted by his actual chances to win.

• If two favorites in a row win, the price on the favorite in the next race will be attractive. Many track birds have the feeling that a long shot is now due and consequently avoid the favorite. This superstition tends to raise the favorite's odds. The odds on the favorite will rise even higher if three or four favorites win in succession. On the other hand, following wins by two consecutive long shots, the odds on the next race's favorite falls below the price warranted by his ability. The race tracksters now feel that the favorite is due.

• Favorites run better on Saturdays than on weekdays. The reason has nothing to do with astrology, so help me Taurus! It's simply that Saturday programs feature the better horses at the track. Better horses mean classier horses and classier horses run more consistently than their colleagues who get weekday billing.

• A horse that has run well at another track is a good bet notwithstanding an off performance his first time out at the track you are visiting. He was simply getting to know the track, and may be ready to resume his winning ways now that he's had a turn around the oval.

• In appraising the past performance charts, pay more attention to a horse's number of lengths off the winner than to whether he finished third, fifth, seventh, or what-have-you.

• When the race is at seven furlongs or less, and where the speed ratings of the competitors were earned at the same track over which they are racing today, and for the same distance over which they are racing today, speed rating handicapping is, by itself, a sound basis for investment.

• Track records are not too meaningful. Many a horse might have broken most of the records on the books had he not been eased up rather than have him strain himself in a race he was going to win anyway. In addition, track records must be viewed critically because of such varying factors as the speed of the track, the number of its turns, the weather, and the whole shebang of qualifications noted by us in our chapter on speed.

● The more firmly packed the dirt, the faster the track. Tracks will also be faster following a long dry spell. This is relevant in terms of the need to be careful not to assume that a horse's time at another track is evidence that it can run to that time again at this track.

● On a muddy field, pick the horse with early speed. The advantage is his because the mud's in the eye of his followers. (No kidding.)

● On muddy tracks, the inside post frequently catches the water drain, making it slower going.

● Generally speaking, eastern tracks are slower than western tracks.

● Bet the horse, not the jockey. The top jock in the world can't climb off his nag and carry him across the finish line. If the horses of your choice are equally matched, then the quality of the jockey becomes important.

● Because many fans are prone to betting the jockey, the mounts of the highest rated jockeys frequently draw lower odds than they merit.

● The inside post is an advantage in sprint races if the horse starting from it is not a comparatively slow breaker. If he is, the faster breaking horses on the outside will box him in. In short, inside post, fast breaker, good bet. However, inside post, slow breaker, look for outside post and fast breaker. However, when all things are equal, bear in mind that the horse with the inside post position has less ground to cover than the horse with an outside post.

● Lay off sprinters in route races. Same, routers in sprint races. However, if there is a long high-class sprinter entered in a route race, look him over carefully. The distance racers may permit the sprinter to set his own pace. If they lay back too far and don't press him, he may just go all the way. Good prices are available in this kind of situation.

● Route distance races are more predictable than sprint races. In the mile and longer races there is time to compensate for a bad start. Also, a horse that finds himself boxed in has the time over the route distance in which to work out his problem. Racing luck in a sprint race, however, can mean sudden death for the bettor.

● The weight factor is more meaningful in distance races than in the sprints. Wonder why? Try carrying fifty pounds for ten yards. Now try it over twenty yards. See what I mean?

● In sprint races class and speed are more important than weight, sex, and age.

● In route races favor horses over colts, and horses and colts over fillies and mares.

● In route races for horses of mixed ages lay off three-year-olds and even four-year-olds during the first half of the year.

● In a route race, if you have narrowed your selection down to two or three horses none of whom have a recent index for the distance to be run, lean to the horse who has had workouts over the longest distance. The horse with the shorter distance workouts is at a conditioning disadvantage. Besides, who knows but that this race is itself intended as that horse's conditioner?

● In a route race, if a horse goes to post with meaningfully more weight that he was assigned, forget him.

● Class is more important than speed. Class is more important than speed. Class is more important than speed. And especially so in route races.

● In races for fillies and mares, all things equal, bet the mare.

● As a rule, in races for thoroughbreds of varied ages, the older animals have the advantage.

● As another rule, stay away from fillies and mares in races that include the menfolk—colts, geldings, and/or horses.

● Top-weight horses are usually the best horses by virtue of their past performance or in the eyes of the racing secretary. They are good show bets.

● Underlays of a precipitous nature are often worth a bettor's fling.

● While entries would appear to give the bettor more of a chance of winning, 'tain't so. Not only ain't it so, but they are almost always overbet by the doggedly naïve public, resulting in their odds being lower than their talent warrants.

● A horse that is showing improvement in its breaks from the post may be trying to tell you that it is ready. I have found this fact a veritable divining rod for selecting long shots—so much so, that I almost hate to tell y'all about it.

● And may the Great Handicapper above forgive me for indiscriminately sharing with one and all the following open sesame to long-shot winners: Watch for the horse who, no matter his unimpressive past performances, has been getting closer and closer to the pace and has shown in his last time out that he was able to stay near contention at the head of the stretch. Never you mind that he never finished the race. Unless his chart shows him to be a chronic quitter, he may be signalling us that he is coming along and is now ready. This one can really pay off!

CHAPTER 12

Pari-Mutuels and the Tote Board

THE TOTALISATOR, a portable assembly of especially designed electrical equipment, registers each bet, issues a ticket as a receipt for the bettor, and totalizes and displays the summations of the wages. What's more, its tapeworm appetite is virtually indigestion-free. The American Totalisator Company, a group of gentlemen who as boys must have been wows at the erector set, proudly allow that the gadget has ingested billions of dollars with inaccuracies limited to 3/10,000 of 1 per cent! How 'bout that?

The tote machine's origins were humble. 'Way back in 1865, when American horse enthusiasts were preoccupied with cavalry doings at Appomatox, one Pierre Oller, a

French perfume shop proprietor, decided to diversify his financial involvements. He got the bright idea of selling tickets on the races and keeping all of the proceeds in a common pool. When pay-off time came, Lucky Pierre cut himself in for a 5 per cent handling charge and distributed the balance to the winners, ratioed to the odds established by his clients' bets. Notwithstanding the anguished cries of bookmakers and lovers of Chanel Number 5, zee French tracks prevailed on Pierre to forego the attar of roses and set up his system on the racing parks' grounds. By 1887 pari (from Paree) mutuel wagering became the legalized betting form in France.

It took fully forty years for the pari-mutuel system of betting to cross the English Channel. And just as an earlier forty-year trek required the direction of a Moses to qualify it for a Mission Accomplished stamp, this one was led by no less a peerless leader than Sir Winston Churchill. In 1927 the English parliament, responsive to Sir Winston's roaratory, passed legislation establishing the totalisator and pari-mutuel betting at all English tracks. Although Sir Winston scolded England's bookies, scapegoating them as a rationale for his legalized gambling bill, if truth be known, in pressing for the pari-mutuel act, Winnie foresaw the ease with which the Empire could siphon needed tax revenues off the totalisator system.

By 1933, the American Totalisator Company installed its machine at Arlington Park, outside of Chicago. In 1939, New York made constitutional provision for pari-mutuel betting, and today you name the track worthy of a thoroughbred, and it employs the system.

What does the tote board, that huge contraption in the infield of the track, the one with all of those numerals, tell us? And how does the pari-mutuel system, to which the tote machine is slavishly dedicated, work? We'll give the latter question a go first, and then we'll more readily dig the tote board.

Without going into the complex electronic machinations involved, suffice it to say that all of the money that the track's patrons bring to the Win cages, the Place cages, and the Show cages are kept in three separate pools. No matter that you frequent the $2, $5, $10, or $100 window or the $6, $15, or $30 Combination window (Combination is formal talk for across-the-board), your win bet is pooled with everybody else's win bet no matter the amount, and the same goes for place and show pools. All the time that this money is accumulating, busy adding machines compute the odds that the public is establishing and then flash these odds onto the tote board. The odds for each pool are established by the amount of money bet on each horse in relation to the total amount of money in the pool, less the state's and track's "take."

By simple illustration, which conveys substantially what happens in the pari-mutuel system, let us assume that two horses, Semper Fidelis and I Got Mine, are competing in a match race. Let us also assume that three fans are betting. Launcelot and Robespierre each bet two dollars on Semper Fidelis. Heathcliff lays two on the nose of I Got Mine. That puts a total of six dollars in the win pool.

One more assumption, now: that the state in which the race is being held has a mutuel take of 10 per cent. Immediately, then, 10 per cent is deducted from the six dollars, leaving the pool with six dollars less sixty cents, or $5.40. With the track and the state now assured, we proceed.

The bugler bugles, the entrants enter, they parade by the clubhouse, they limber up, they reach the post, they're in the starting gate, the red flag drops, and they're off! The track announcer makes like he's reporting the Charge of the Light Brigade, and naturally nobody hears a damn thing. When it's all over, the bright yellow silks of I Got Mine cross the finish line four lengths in front of the true-blue colors of Semper Fidelis.

Heathcliff's luck has finally changed. His was the winning ticket.

Meanwhile, back at the control room, man and machine have already figured out what Heathcliff's win is going to mean to him in terms of the stuff for which grocers ex-

change their wares. They have set aside the amount of
money that was bet on I Got Mine, determined how much
was now available for distribution, and flashed the result
to the board in the infield. The result: $5.40. How come?
It consists of Heathcliff's original two-dollar investment
plus the remaining money ($3.40) in the pool. (It's really
somewhat more complex than this, but basically this is
what happens. Students seeking extra credit may see me
after class for more details.)

Now we are ready for a look at the face of the tote
machine, namely and to wit, the tote board. Or, as
grandma, bless her stodgy heart, always calls it, the
Totalisator Board. Here is an illustration of a typical
board.

The pictured American Totalisator Display Board is
the double-wing type. The two wings are the panels on
the extreme right and on the extreme left, which provide
identical information for the fans who are dispersed from
the clubhouse area in front of the finish line and for those
'way over at the beginning of the stretch where the grandstand area usually begins. The outside panels, the ones
that read OFFICIAL, tell us that a race has just been run
and the results are now official. For instance, we know
that the number 3 horse (every horse on the racing program has a number for betting purposes) finished first
and paid $8.60 to win, $3.80 to place, and $3.00 to show.
Also revealed is the information on the identity of the
horses that finished second (the number 6 horse), third
(the number 4 horse), and fourth (the number 7 horse).
The place horse paid $4.00 to place and $3.00 for the
show position. The show horse paid $5.60. All pay-off
prices are based on a two-dollar bet. In addition, this
panel tells us the post time, the time of day at the moment, and the time of the winning horse.

The next panel, the one to the immediate right of the
extreme left panel and the one to the immediate left of
the extreme right panel, tells us the number of the race
(it was the first race) and on this particular tote board,
the condition of the track (it was good). Also, and im-

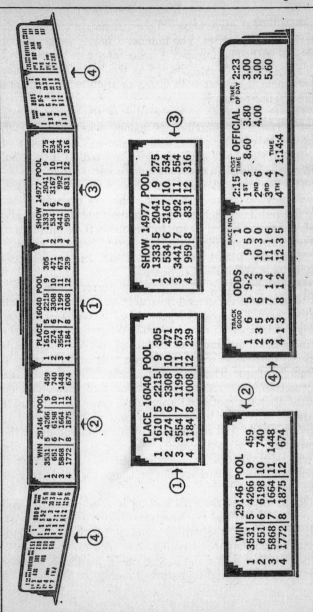

portantly, this panel shows the approximate closing odds on the twelve entries. The number 1 horse, we see, went off at 6 to 1. The number 3 horse who won went off at 3 to 1. ($8.60, his win price, less the bettor's two-dollar investment leaves us with $6.60, or slightly more than a three-to-one return.)

The three panels in the center of the pictured tote board reveal the amount of money wagered on each entrant to win, to place, and to show. The amount of money at the top of each of these three panels is the total amount of money in that particular pool.

The figures on the odds panels and on the win, place, and show pool panels blink the changes brought about by the public's betting. These changes are automatically relayed to the board by the totalisator in the control room every ninety seconds during the period between races.

Now, my friend, you know about the pari-mutuel system and about the tote board.

Here's something about which you may not know.

Have you ever noticed how neat and even the pay-off prices are? The price may be $4.40 or $5.80 or $14.00. Never $4.49 or $5.88 or $14.07. What happens to the hundreds of thousands of dollars of left-over odd cents during the course of a year? Lean over and I'll tell you what happens. These pennies, called "breakage," are deemed by the racing associations and the sovereign states to be a potential source of annoyance to track patrons. All those loose pennies and nickels jingling in one's pockets! And so, burning with consideration for the convenience of said patrons, meaning we peasants, the tracks and Der State, with a spirit of service that is spelled G-R-E-E-D, pocket the breakage for us. How nice can people be?

Well, anyway, the pari-mutuel system of betting and the development of the totalisator board are as responsible as anything mechanical could be for the wide popularity of thoroughbred racing. And also for the remarkable confidence that the racing public justifiably reposes in the on-the-up-and-up nature of racing.

CHAPTER 13

How to Read the Dope

To THE UNINITIATED who chance a confrontation with the *Daily Racing Form*, the text may seem formidable. All those numbers, fractions, abbreviations, doodads, and what not!

Actually, however, it's easy reading. Look at some of the Runyonesque *literati* of the form, and you'll assume with safety that the past performances and racing charts are no more a reading strain than the fare in a barbershop magazine rack.

In this chapter we will prove this. We will guide the reader through a step-by-step reading course on the Result Charts and the Past Performances, as they appear in the *Daily Racing Form*.

As a matter of fact, got two bits? It can get you a copy of "How to Read Charts and Past Performances." Honest injun, it can. The *Daily Racing Form* people will send the booklet to you for that pittance. You can get yours from any of the *Daily Racing Form's* conveniently located offices in New York City, Los Angeles, Chicago, Seattle, Toronto, or Miami.

Still, on the chance that you figure you've spent enough on this tome without getting in deeper, here goes with our own reading course. First, the result chart.

Whereas the past performances provide the details on a group of past races in which the horses currently matched against each other had competed, the result charts tell the story of a single race, and how its cast behaved.

Here's the illustration:

THIRD RACE

Keystone

FEBRUARY 17, 1979

6 FURLONGS. (1.08⅖) CLAIMING. Purse $8,000. Fillies, 3-year-old, weights, 122 lbs. Non-winners of two races since December 17, allowed 2 lbs. A race since then, 4 lbs. A race since December 10, 6 lbs. Claiming price $11,000 for each $500 to $9,000, 1 lb. (Races where entered for $8,500 or less not considered in estimating allowances).

Value of race $8,000, value to winner $4,800, second $1,600, third $880, fourth $480, fifth $240. Mutuel pool $47,724. Exacta Pool $69,887.

Last Raced	Horse	Eqt. A. Wt	PP St	¼	½	Str	Fin	Jockey	Cl'g Pr	Odds $1
31Jan79 ⁵Key¹	Herby Costa	3 116	4 2	1½	1½	1¹½	1½	Gomez M A	11000	9.50
26Jan79 ²Key³	Anita's Girl	b 3 116	1 6	6½	3¹	3¹½	2⁴	Pagano S R	11000	3.10
19Jan79 ⁵Key⁴	Dollies Cabin	b 3 116	3 7	7	4¹½	4²	3½	Nied J Jr	11000	3.10
4Feb79 ⁴Key³	Miss Info	3 112	7 3	3ʰᵈ	5¹	5⁴	4¹	Klidzia S³	10000	5.10
16Jan79 ⁷Key¹	Little Peach	3 116	5 1	2⁶	2⁴	2¹	5⁴	Mucciolo J	10000	3.10
26Jan79 ¹Key¹	Morning Karen	3 108	2 5	5ʰᵈ	6½	6¹	6³	Marshall L¹⁰	11000·	17.90
29Dec78 ⁹Key¹	Nana's Lullaby	3 109	6 4	4½	7	7	7	Trebino A P⁷	11000	4.90

OFF AT 1:35 EST. Start good for all but DOLLIES CABIN. Won driving. Time, :23⅖, :48⅘, 1:16⅗ Track fast.

$2 Mutuel Prices:

4—HERBY COSTA	21.00	7.00	3.00
1—ANITA'S GIRL		4.40	2.40
3—DOLLIES CABIN			2.80
$2 EXACTA 4—1 PAID $108.80.		

Ch. f, by Hansom Harve—Thirsty Princess, by Career Boy. Trainer Euster Eugene. Bred by Sonny Acres Farm (NJ).

HERBY COSTA set the early pace from the inside, drew clear after shaking off LITTLE PEACH in upper stretch and was hard ridden to hold off ANITA'S GIRL. The latter, allowed to settle early, advanced from the inside into stretch, came outside of winner in upper stretch and was slowly getting to that one in late stages. DOLLIES CABIN stumbled badly at the start going to her nose, raced outside of rivals at a lost of ground when improving position on turn and lacked a stretch punch. MISS INFO had no apparent mishap LITTLE PEACH forced the early issue outside of HERBY COSTA but gave way in upper stretch.

Owners— 1, Elgart C; 2, Faust & Glorioso; 3, Lehman E; 4, Fallon M L; 5, Timberland Stable; 6, McCarthy W E; 7, Thompson Jaquelin.

Trainers— 1, Euster Eugene; 2, Glorioso Patricia A; 3, Lehman Edward; 4, Fallon Martin L; 5, Lopez Daniel J; 6, McCarthy William E; 7, Mourar Buck K.

Overweight: Miss Info 1 pound; Little Peach 2; Morning Karen 2.

THIRD RACE

Keystone

February 17, 1979

This means that the race being described is the third race at Keystone on February 17, 1979.

By now you know that a furlong is an eighth of a mile and that 6 *furlongs* means that the race described was three quarters of a mile.

The purse was $8,000 and in straightforward English we learn that it was for three-year-old fillies, assigned 122 lbs. But—watch this—if they haven't been doing all that well, they're entitled to weight off. Haven't won two races in the past two months? Take 2 lbs. off the 122. Not even one win? Take 4 lbs. off.

We know about claiming. This race is for an $11,000 sale price. If an owner were to enter his horse at a bargain price, say $10,500, he'd be entitled to take a pound off. For $10,000, two lbs., and so on, down to the fire-sale price of $9,000.

Still with it? Let's go on.

Value to winner, $4,800; to the place horse, $1,600; to the show horse, $880. Fourth place earned Miss Info $480, and fifth place earned Little Peach $240. The betting public provided the mutuel pool with $47,724 and the exacta pool with $69,887.

Next we come to the chart itself. Note the figure 5 perched on the left shoulder of *Key*. It means that last time out Herby Costa ran in the fifth race at Keystone. The *1* perched on *Key's* right shoulder means she won then too.

The horses' names are listed in the order in which they finished the race. Herby Costa won, wire to wire. Anita's Girl placed, Dollies Cabin showed, and so on down the line to Nana's Lullaby, who finished last.

Eqt is an abbreviation for equipment. The *b* that appears next to the names of the place and show horses means that they were wearing blinkers. Unless otherwise indicated, the jockeys were using whips. An *s* would mean that the rider was equipped with spurs. *A* tells us the age of the horses and inasmuch as the conditions for this race specified three-year-olds, all are noted as *3*.

Wt simply means the weight the horse carried.

PP means post position. Herby Costa started from post position 4. The post positions are drawn by lot.

Next we see columns headed by *St, ¼, ½, Str, Fin*. These terms mean, respectively, start, quarter mile call, half mile call, position of the horse in the stretch, and at the finish. Inasmuch as the charts read differently from the past performances, let us read across with the horse Dollies Cabin, the show horse in this race.

See the 7 in the column headed *St?* The 7 indicates that Dollies Cabin broke in seventh position. Under the column headed ¼, Dollies Cabin still shows 7; she is, in fact, still last. But at ½, she seems to be coming alive. Note now the figure $4^{1\frac{1}{2}}$. This means that after half a mile, Dollies Cabin is in fourth place, one and a half lengths (1½) ahead of fifth place Miss Info. Reread that line. Note that I said that the *1½* means that Dollies Cabin was leading Miss Info by that much. If this were a past performance chart, the figure over the shoulder of the number telling the position of the horse would indicate numbers of lengths off the lead horse. In the result charts, however, the shoulder-perching figure reveals the distance by which the horse leads the horse behind. In the stretch call Dollies Cabin is still running in fourth place, but now two lengths ahead of Miss Info.

To determine how far Dollies Cabin is from the nose of the lead horse at any given call, simply add the lengths noted on the shoulder of the positions of the horses ahead of her. For instance, in the stretch Herby Costa is leading by ½, Little Peach is in second place by 1, and Anita's Girl is third by 1½. Add ½ to 1 to 1½ and we know that fourth place Dollies Cabin trails Herby Costa in the stretch by 4 lengths. Further, we know that although Dollies Cabin finished the race third it isn't so much that she was gaining ground as it was that Little Peach was fading. How do we know that? By noting that at the finish, Herby Costa was first by ½ length and Anita's Girl second by 4 lengths. Actually, Dollies Cabin was half a length closer in the stretch, when she was in fourth place!

Easy? Sure it is.

The column *Jockey* isn't going to be explained, except for the figures over Klidzia, Marshall, and Trebino. Those figures are weight allowances for these apprentice jockeys.

The final column is *Odds $1*. In this column is listed the odds to $1.00 at which the horses left the post. Herby Costa went off at $9.50 to $1.00. These odds can be readily determined by subtracting the $2.00 paid for the mutuel ticket from the win price and dividing the remainder in half. For instance, Herby Costa paid $21.00 to win. Subtract the two-dollar investment and you have left $19.00. Divide the $19.00 in half and you've got $9.50.

Sometimes you'll see an *a* in front of the *Odds $1* line for two horses. This means that these two horses are an "entry," that is, that they are either owned by one party, or if owned by separate parties, are nonetheless trained by a single trainer. A mutuel ticket on either horse will pay off no matter which of the two wins. If there are two sets of entries in a race, an *a* and a *b* will appear before the *Odds $1* figure on their lines.

Sometimes the *Odds $1* line will show an *f* for a horse or horses. The *f* will mean that the horse so described is in the "mutuel field." The mutuel field includes the horses in the post positions beyond the number 12. These are the horses running from positions for which the pari-mutuel machines are not equipped to handle bets. A winning ticket on a horse in the mutuel field will pay off even if another horse in the mutuel field may have actually run in the money.

Now, to return to the pictured chart illustration.

Centered under the chart, see the line *Time, :23⅘, :48⅖, 1:16⅗ Track fast*. We discussed this in the chapter on pace. Look it up. You'll remember it better for going to the trouble.

Next, below, is the bold lettering, $2 MUTUEL PRICES. Here we see the win, place, and show pay-off prices for two dollars on the horses that won, placed, and showed. The numbers preceding the names of the horses (4-Herby Costa, 1-Anita's Girl, 3-Dollies Cabin) are the official program numbers that are used to identify the horses for betting purposes.

Ch. f, by Hansom Harve—Thirty Princess, by Career Boy tells us that Herby Costa, the winning horse, is a chestnut (Ch) filly (f) whose sire was Hansom Harve and whose dam was Thirsty Princess, and that Thirsty Princess' sire was Career Boy. This information is known as the winner's breeding.

Trainer Euster Eugene. Bred by Sonny Acres Farm (NJ). Any questions on that?

The rest of the copy is self-explanatory, being a detailed description of the race, and a listing of all the owners and trainers in the cast.

Overweight tells us that the jockeys atop the noted horses weighed 1, 2, and 3 pounds, respectively, more than the weight allowed the horses.

So much for result charts. Now to the past performances, with which the average bettor will have more frequent occasion to do business.

Much of the technique of reading the past performances has already been discussed in the foregoing text. However, as a wrap-up, and also because we have not considered all of the items carried in the past performances, we'll run through a sample form. Here it is:

Men's Lad — **Ch. g. 4, by Quid Pro Quo—Men Mad, by Bold Lad**
$11,500 **Br.—Paxson Mrs H D (Md)**
Own.—Mendelson E — **Tr.—Alfano Ronald A**

10Feb79-7Bow	fst	1 1/16	:49⅘	1:14⅗	1:49⅗	Clm 11500	5	2	3½	2½	3^{1}	2^{nk}	Baker C J^{5}
29Jan79-6Bow	fst	1 1/16	:49⅕	1:14⅕	1:48⅗	Clm 9500	3	3	$3^{2½}$	$2^{1½}$	2^{hd}	1^{nk}	Miceli M
20Jan79-2Bow	sly	1 1/16	:48	1:13⅕	1:45⅗	Clm 11500	3	9	$9^{8½}$	$9^{8¾}$	9^{11}	8^{11}	Miceli M
5Jan79-7Bow	fst	1 1/16	:47	1:12⅕	1:45	Clm 14500	2	6	8^{18}	7^{14}	7^{10}	7^{14}	Miceli M
26Dec78-8Med	fst	1 1/16	:47⅗	1:12⅗	1:45⅗	Clm 14000	1	7	$7^{7½}$	$6^{7½}$	$4^{6½}$	2^{7}	Miceli M
8Dec78-5Med	sly	1^{70}	:47⅗	1:13⅘	1:45⅘	Clm 14000	4	5	5^{7}	5^{3}	$5^{6½}$	$3^{9½}$	Miceli M
30Nov78-2Med	sly	1 1/16	:47	1:12⅘	1:46⅗	Clm 12500	1	5	6^{11}	5^{3}	1½	$1^{1½}$	Miceli M
17Nov78-9Med	sly	6^{f}	:22⅕	:45⅗	1:12⅕	Clm c-10000	10	2	7^{11}	6^{12}	5^{7}	$4^{2¼}$	Arellano J
10Nov78-5Med	fst	6^{f}	:22⅘	:46⅗	1:12	3↑Clm 9000	4	5	$6^{3¼}$	7^{8}	$4^{2½}$	1½	Arellano J
11Aug78-6Mth	gd	1 1/16	:47	1:12⅗	1:45⅘	Clm 11000	7	10	10^{11}	$10^{8¾}$	$10^{9¼}$	9^{15}	Arellano J

Turf Record	St.	1st	2nd	3rd			St.	1st	2nd	3rd	Amt.
119	1	0	0	0		1979	4	1	1	0	$6,970
						1978	21	5	2	2	$32,690

b 114	6.80	59–31	Ballroom Dancer 114^{nk} Men's Lad 114^{1} Fortent 104^{3}	Altered course	9
b 112	9.90	63–30	Men's Lad 112^{nk} Laudo $107^{1¼}$ Pocotaligo 107^{4}	Driving	8
b 114	*2.60	67–21	Port Conway Lane 114¾ Ballroom Dancer 114^{3} Fortent 114¾	Outrun	9
b 119	5.80	67–23	Annuitant 105^{4} Prime Hour 114½ Telex Number 108^{nk}	Outrun	8
b 112	7.30	76–18	Traffic Host 108^{7} Men's Lad 112^{6} Constitution Hill 111^{nk}	Rallied	8
112	*1.40	62–28	Johnny And Joey $116^{1½}$ Princely Glory 116^{8} Men's Lad 112½	No threat	6
b 116	3.90	79–22	Men's Lad $116^{1½}$ Mr. Eldag 116^{7} Stokesy Boy 116no	Driving	8
b 119	5.80	82–20	Bold Brawler 116^{nk} Silver Pedlar 107^{hd} Goodbye Folks 109^{2}	Rallied	10
b 112	26.40	85–17	Men's Lad 112½ Alishamar 111^{hd} Bland Distinctive 109^{3}	Driving	8
b 116	6.60	61–18	Heavy Iron 114^{hd} Positive Binn 116^{6} Freedom Bell $116^{3¾}$	Outrun	10

LATEST WORKOUTS **Jan 16 Bow 6f fst 1:18⅕ b** **Dec 22 Med 7f gd 1:30⅖ b**

Men's Lad is the name of the horse.
ch. g. 4, by Quid Pro Quo—Men Mad, by Bold Lad
$11,500 *Br.—Paxson Mrs H D (Md)*
Tr. Alfano Ronald A 119

The figure 119 tells us the amount of weight Men's Lad is carrying today; Men's Lad is a chestnut (ch) gelding (g), four years old, and his sire is Quid Pro Quo. He's the get of Men Mad (helluva name for a broodmare, isn't it?), who in turn was sired by Bold Lad. Mrs. Paxson, of Maryland, is the breeder and Ronald Alfano is the trainer.

Incidentally, chestnuts vary from light to dark and can be distinguished from bays by their tails and manes. Chestnuts don't have black tails and manes. Chestnut-looking bays do—and so they're bays. Bays range from a light yellowy tan to a near brown. Brown would be abbreviated "br"; "blk" is for black. Gray horses are "gr" and roans are "ro."

Under Men's Lad, *Own* tells us that his room and board is paid for by one E. Mendelson. Now let your eye move to the right. The figure $11,500 tells us that the race we are trying to dope out is an $11,500 claiming race. The figures beside 1979 and 1978, as we have noted in our text, are the numbers of starts made by Men's Lad in those years (4 and 21, respectively) and the number of times the horse has won, placed, and showed. The amount of dollars tells us that in 1979 Men's Lad's purses up until this particular race totalled $6,970. In 1978 it was $32,690.

We are now ready for the body of the past performance chart. Reading from left to right, we start with *10 Feb 79- 7 Bow fst* $1\frac{1}{16}$. This tells us that the last time the horse raced was on February 10th, 1979, in the seventh race at Bowie. The track was fast that day and the distance was a mile and a sixteenth. The time before that, he raced at the same track, on January 29th in the sixth race, also at the mile and a sixteenth distance. He's raced at Meadowlands (Med) and at Monmouth (Mth) in his last ten efforts. The past performance charts list a horse's last ten races.

The following three columns (returning to 10Feb79) read: 49⅘ 1:14⅖ 1:49⅖. This tells us that the horse that won that race covered the mile and a sixteenth in one minute, forty-nine and two-fifth seconds. Further, that

the lead horse at the end of half a mile was clocked in
49⅗ seconds, and the lead horse at the end of three
quarters of a mile was clocked at 1:14⅖ seconds. To determine Men's Lad's time we add a fifth of a second for
each length by which he trailed the leader.

Note *Turf Record* to the left of Men's Lad's 1979 and
1978 win, place, and show record. For all that he's raced
25 times, he has tried the turf but once, and without
placing. Were he partial to grass, his past performance
record would show ⓣ indicating that a given outing
was on the grass. Track conditions for turf races are
noted as *fm*, telling us the grass was firm, or as *sf*, for
soft footing. Men's Lad is raced on dirt and his last two
races were on fast tracks (*fst*), but on January 20 at
Bowie he found a sloppy (*sly*) track, and on August 11th,
1978, a good (*gd*) track—one not fast but faster than
slow (*sl*) or muddy (*m*) or heavy (*hy*).

Following the claiming price for which he ran on
February 10th, we see 5 2 3½ 2½ 3[1] 2[nk]. As discussed in the
text, these are the positions of Men's Lad at the various
calls. He broke second from post position 5 and at the
first call the gelding was third, trailing the front horse by
half a length (3½); at the next call Men's Lad had moved
into second place, still trailing the leader by a half length
(2½). In the stretch he was third, a length off the leader
(3[1]), and at the wire he failed by a neck (2[nk]).

Baker CJ[5] tells us the name of the boy who was "up"
and that he was entitled to a five pound apprentice advantage. Said otherwise, the figure *114* following Baker's
name would have been 119 but for Baker's apprentice
standing. The *b* advises us that Men's Lad wore blinkers.

See the number *6.80* to the right of *114*? That was the
odds at which Men's Lad left the post. On January 20th
when he raced eighth, losing by eleven lengths, his odds
were 2.60 to 1. The asterisk preceding the 2.60 means
that he was the favorite. Some favorite! If you should find
an *e* following the odds in a past performance chart of a
horse you are handicapping, it does not mean a star for
effort. It does mean that the horse was part of an entry.

Now let's return to the column from which we gather the kind of company Men's Lad has been keeping—the column that tells us this is a claiming horse whose last race was for an $11,500 price. Note that when on November 17th he ran at Meadowland (Med) for $10,000, the figure is preceded by a *c*. That means that he was claimed on that day and Mr. Mendelson has owned him ever since.

Remember our discussion of speed ratings? That's what the column following the odds is all about. Men's Lad's last speed rating was 59. Bad? Not good, but given that we're dealing with a cheap plater, he's better than the 59 suggests—and we know it from the figure *31* which is coupled with 59. Let your eyedrop down over the gelding's previous races. See his speed ratings for like distances. They're better. But something else is evident. The companion figures are lower. The reason for this is that the companion figure tells us how fast the races were being run that day by all the horses competing. If, because the track was very fast, or very slow, we get an insight into the speed rating, it can only help us in our handicapping today. The faster the track (or the higher the quality of horses), the lower will the companion figure be. The slower the track (or the quality of the competition), the higher the companion figure.

Given this fact, note that Men's Lad's 59 is the poorest speed rating he's had. However, the 31 suggests that on February 10th he raced over the slowest of the tracks for his last ten races. When the track speed quotient was 18 (December 26th, Meadowlands) Men's Lad's speed rating was 76!

While we have discussed the common types of races, there are a few that the reader may occasionally see abbreviated in his racing form, and lest he grow frantic for not having been adequately briefed, here goes: *Mdn* means that the race is one for maidens. Maidens in horse-talk means non-winners, regardless of their sex. A notation *M14000* would mean that the race is a claiming race at $14,000 for maidens. *Mtch* tells us that the race is a match race—that is, one in which two horses are competing, A15000 would mean that the race is a "starter allowance" one. This means that the event is being run under allowance conditions with horses who have previously started for the noted claiming price or less as stated in the conditions. An A15000 race suggests that the horses must have run for a claiming price of $15,000 or less. In these starter races the horses are not subject to claim, it being basically an allowance race. °10,000 would mean that we are looking at a race that was a $10,000 optional claiming race and that the horse in question was entered *not* to be claimed. $10,000° would mean that the race was a $10,000 optional claiming race and that the horse was entered to be claimed.

Finally, we note *Ballroom Dancer 114ⁿᵏ Men's Lad 114¹ Fortent 104³ Altered course 9.* This so-called "best company line" informs us who won that race and what weight he carried and by how much he led his immediate pursuer. *Altered course* is not the name of the fourth horse. It is the form's capsule comment designed to help us. Indeed, over a like track and over the same distance, Men's Lad ran 4 lengths slower on February 10th than he did on January 29th. "Altered course" suggests the reason.

Last, at the very bottom of the past performance chart, we see *Latest Workouts—Jan 16 Bow 6f fst 1:18½b.* By now, all of this save the *b* is readily understood by faithful readers. What means the *b*? The *b* means that in his workout the horse worked "breezing." He might have been noted as having done the five furlongs in a given time followed by an *h* which would have meant he covered the distance "handily," or with a *d* for "driving" or with an *e* for "easily or with an *o* for "all out." A *u* would mean that he "eased up," a *g* that the horse worked from the gate, a *bo* that he "bore out," and an *ro* that he "ran out."

That's it, folks.

If you have read through this chapter you should feel some satisfaction.

You have proven that you've got the makings of a successful horse-player. Many of your co-purchasers of this minor classic finished reading the main text and ran like hell to the nearest horse-playing emporium. They are hasty of mind and the kind that Lady Fate selects as her patsies. I wish them luck. They may need it. You? You are the footnote readers of our hurry-hurry society. Yours are life's spoils. You are the track's counterparts of the judiciary's painstaking opinion writers, the counterpart not of the men who dream of castles, but of those who build them. And on the off chance that for all of your thoroughness you are nonetheless destined to be a loser, yours to solace you is the balm of *losing knowledgeably*. No small thing, that.

Appendix

THE FOLLOWING is a listing of North American tracks and their abbreviations as carried in *The Daily Racing Form*. The tracks marked with an asterisk (*) are less than a mile in circumference. When comparing the chances of a world-beater in Albuquerque, New Mexico, against a so-so horse from Saratoga, look out!

AC	— (Agua) Caliente, Mexico	GF	—*Great Falls, Montana
Aks	— Ak-Sar-Ben, Omaha, Neb.	GG	— Golden Gate Fields, Cal.
Alb	— Albuquerque, N. Mexico	GM	—*Green Mountain, Vermont
AP	— Arlington Park, Illinois	GP	— Gulfstream Park, Florida
Aqu	— Aqueduct, New York	Grd	—*Greenwood, Can.
AsD	—*Assiniboia D'ns, Win'g, Can.	GS	— Garden State Park, N. J.
Atl	—*Atlantic City, N. Jersey	Haw	— Hawthorne, Illinois
Ato	—*Atokad Pk., S. Sioux C., Neb.	Hia	— Hialeah Park, Fla.
BB	—*Blue Bonnets, Canada	Hol	— Hollywood Park, Cal.
BD	—*Berkshire Downs, Mass.	HP	—*Hazel Park, Michigan
Bel	— Belmont Park, New York	JnD	—*Jefferson Downs, La.
Beu	— Beulah Park, Ohio	Jua	— Juarez, Mexico
BF	—*Brockton Fair, Mass.	Kee	— Keeneland, Kentucky
Bil	—*Billings, Montana	Key	— Keystone Race Track, Pa.
BM	— Bay Meadows, California	LA	—*Los Alamitos, California
BmF	— Bay Meadows Fair, Cal.	LaD	— Louisiana Downs, La.
Bml	— Balmoral, Illinois	LaM	—*La Mesa P'k, Rat'n, N. Mex.
Boi	—*Boise, Idaho	Lat	— Latonia, Kentucky
Bow	—*Bowie, Maryland	Lbg	—*Lethbridge, Alberta, Can.
CD	— Churchill Downs, Ky.	LD	—*Lincoln Downs, R. I.
CDA	—*Coeur d'Alene, Idaho	Lga	—*Longacres, Washington
Ceg	—*Calgary, Alberta, Can.	LnN	—*Lincoln State Fair, Neb.
Cen	— Centennial Race Tr'k, Colo.	Lrl	— Laurel Race Course, Md.
Cka	—*Cahokia Downs, Illinois	MD	—*Marquis Downs, Can.
Cls	—*Columbus, Nebraska	Med	— Meadowlands, N. J.
Com	—*Commodore Downs, Pa.	Mex	—*Mexico City, Mexico
Crc	— Calder Race Course, Fla.	MF	—*Marshfield Fair, Mass.
CT	—*Charles Town, W. Va.	MP	—*Miles Park, Kentucky
Cwl	—*Commonwealth, Ky.	Mth	— Monmouth Park, N. J.
	Formerly Miles Park	Nar	— Narragansett Park, R. I.
DeD	—*Delta Downs, La.	Nmp	—*Northampton, Mass.
Del	— Delaware Park, Delaware	NP	—*Northlands Park, Canada
Det	— Detroit, Michigan	OP	— Oaklawn Park, Arkansas
Dmr	— Del Mar, California	Pen	— Penn National, Pa.
EIP	— Ellis Park, Kentucky	Pim	— Pimlico, Maryland
EP	—*Exhibit'n Pk., B. C., Can.	PJ	—*Park Jefferson, S. D.
EvD	—*Evangeline Downs, La.	Pla	—*Playfair, Washington
FD	— Florida Downs, Fla.	Pln	— Pleasanton, California
FE	— Fort Erie, Canada	PM	— Portland Meadows, Ore.
Fer	— Ferndale, California	Pmf	— Portl'nd M'd'ws Fair, Ore.
FG	— Fair Grounds, N. Orleans, La.	Poc	—*Pocono Downs, Pa.
FL	— Finger Lakes, Can'gua, N. Y.	Pom	— Pomona, California
Fno	— Fresno, California	PR	— Puerto Rico (El Com'te)
Fon	—*Fonner Park, Nebraska	Pre	—*Prescott Downs, Ariz.
FP	—*Fairmount Park, Illinois	RaP	—*Raceway Pk., Toledo, O.
GBF	—*Great Barrington, Mass.	RD	— River Downs, Ohio

Reg	—*Regina, Canada	SR	—*Santa Rosa, California
Ril	—*Rillito, Arizona	Stk	— Stockton, California
Rkm	— Rockingham Park, N. H.	Stp	—*Stampede Park, Alberta, Can.
Rui	—*Ruidoso, New Mexico	Suf	— Suffolk Downs, Mass.
SA	— Santa Anita Park, Cal.	Sun	—*Sunland Park, New Mex.
Sac	— Sacramento, California	Tdn	— Thistledown, Ohio
Sal	—*Salem, Ore. (Lone Oak)	Tim	—*Timonium, Maryland
San	—*Sandown P'k., B. C., Can.	TuP	— Turf Paradise, Arizona
Sar	— Saratoga Springs, N. Y.	Was	— Washington Park, Ill.
SFe	—*Santa Fe, New Mexico	Wat	— Waterford Park, W. Va.
ShD	—*Shenand'h Downs, W. Va.	Wey	—*Weymouth Fair, Mass.
Sol	—*Solano, California	WO	— Woodbine, Canada
Spt	—*Sportsman's Park, Ill.	YM	— Yakima Meadows, Wash.

GLOSSARY

Across the board   A bet placed on a horse to win, place, and show. It pays for all three positions if the horse wins; if the horse places, it pays for the place and show position; if the horse shows, it pays only for the show bet.

Apprentice jockey   An apprentice jockey is one who is between the ages of 16 and 25, was not at any time a licensed jockey, who is under contract to an owner or trainer for 3 to 5 years, and who has served for a year with a racing stable. Thereupon he is eligible for a 5-pound allowance (except in handicaps) until he has ridden 40 winners. He retains this allowance for a year even though he may reach a total of 40 winners prior to the elapse of a year. For the year afterward he may claim a 3-pound allowance, provided he is riding for his original contract employer.

Backstretch   The straightaway between the end of the clubhouse turn and the beginning of the far turn.

Bar shoes   Worn over the hoof in order to protect a quarter crack or other hoof ailment.

Blaze   A patch of white hair, larger than a "star" on the horse's forehead.

Bog spavin   Swelling on inside, front of hock, resulting from overwork.

Bone spavin   Growth inside and below hock joint, resulting from concussion or strain. Can cause lameness.

Boots and Saddle   Bugler's call signifying that horses have left the walking ring.

Bowed tendon A rupture of the sheath that encloses the flexor tendon extending from the knee to fetlock joint. A serious disability.

Boy Jockey; rider.

Breakage A pay-off price of $6.30 may likely be an approximation of the real odds. The mathematics of the odds may have warranted a pay-off price of $6.34. The four cents, retained by the track and or state, is breakage.

Breeder Owner of the dam that has given birth to the get.

Breezing A term used to describe a workout in which the horse is running under a hold, and has as yet to extend himself to full speed.

Broken wind Breakdown of the air vesicles of the lungs. Results from strain or excessive feeding before exercise.

Brood mare A mare used for breeding purposes.

Brushing Fetlock injury caused by a kick from the opposite foot.

Bucked shins An inflammation of the periosteum on the front of the cannon bone. Commonly found in younger animals.

By A term used to identify the sire of a horse, as in Cyane by Turn-To. Turn-To is Cyane's sire.

Calks Metal grips affixed to the front shoes of racers to help them on muddy tracks, and in the case of some horses, on the grass.

Canker A softening of the horn of the hoof: it emits a foul odor.

Capped hock Results from a horse's kicking or rubbing his own hocks while in the stall.

Chestnut A growth on the inside of a horse's leg. There are various shapes of chestnuts and because no two chestnuts within any one shape type are assumed to have the same area in square centimeters, chestnuts serve as a kind of fingerprint for identification purposes.

Clerk of the scales Official who supervises weighing of jockey prior to race and "weighing in" jockey following the race. Also supervises lot drawings for post positions.

Clocker Person who times the morning workouts of horses. He reports his clockings to the racing secretary and to the public handicappers, thereby providing the bettor with meaningful information for handicapping purposes.

Dam Horse's mother.

Dead heat A race in which two or more contestants finish in a tie. Dead heats can result for the win or the place or the show position or for fourth place money. When horses finish in a dead heat for first place, they share the win and place money.

Dirt The course over which most races are run. A dirt course is distinguished from the grass or turf course inside the dirt course.

Dropping weight A horse that is carrying less weight than he did in his last race is dropping weight.

Entry Commonly, all competitors in a race are entrants. However, the term also has special application to two or more horses that are entered in a race and are either owned by the same owner or trained by the same trainer.

False quarter Horizontal crack in the hoof caused by an injury to the coronet.

Far turn The turn out of the backstretch.

Field The totalisator equipment is geared for a maximum of twelve horses. The horses in excess of twelve in a race are designated as the mutuel field. A bet on the number 12 horse pays off if any horse in the field wins. For instance, if fifteen horses were competing, a win by number 12 or by number 13, number 14, or number 15 would be a win for the ticket holders of number 12.

Floating The leveling off of the horse's teeth, for the purpose of improving his chewing.

Foal A male or female newborn horse.

Get A newborn offspring.

Groom Person who cares for horses in the stable.

Grunting A horse that grunts may be unsound in the wind.

Hand   Measurement of height of horses. Equivalent to four inches.

In the money   A horse that either wins, places, or shows is in the money.

Index   A reference to the horse's previous races. Also, a recent index means that the horse has raced recently. An old index means he's not been active for some time.

Infield   The area inside the dirt oval.

Jockey Club   Source of the rules of racing that prevail in the United States and which, by and large, are enforced by the various state racing commissions. Also, keeper of the Stud Book in which is registered every American thoroughbred. Without a certification of registration from the Jockey Club, a horse may not be raced at an American track recognized by a state racing commission.

Knee spavin   Bony growth at the back of the knee and on the inner side. Results from blow or strain. Can be serious.

Laminitus   Inflammation of the sensitive parts under the horny wall of the foot. Serious disease.

Lead pony   The horse that may be seen accompanying racers to the post. The lead pony is an animal known to the nervous racer and serves to quiet the racer.

Length   Measuring distance used to describe the space between horses in competition.

Lugging in   The tendency of a horse to run toward the rail.

Minus pool   A minimum of ten cents per two-dollar winning bet must be paid on winning tickets. When the betting is so concentrated on a single horse as to result in odds that return a pay-off price of less than ten cents per two dollars, the pool is termed a minus pool. When this happens the track makes up the difference between the pool and ten cents per two dollars.

Morning line   The odds at which the track's "price-maker" estimates the horses will leave the post. The morning line odds are listed in the track's program and are noted on the tote board prior to each race.

Navicular disease A corrosive ulcer on the navicular bone, usually in the forefeet. Common. Frequently fatal.

Osselets Bony growth on fetlock or ankle joint, resulting from inflammation of enveloping membrane of the bone, due to injuries.

Outrider The uniformed rider who accompanies the horses to the post.

Over the grass A race on the turf is over the grass.

Paddock An enclosure for horses. At the track, the enclosure in which the horses are saddled, and where they are identified by the paddock judge to be certain that they are the horses actually entered in the race.

Paddock judge Has supervisory responsibility for horses in the paddock area prior to their leaving for the post parade. Also, identifies horses to ascertain whether they are in fact the horses that have been entered in the race.

Past performances The records and accounts of a thoroughbred's races.

Patrol judge Once the race is in progress, the horses are under the close scrutiny of patrol judges who are stationed around the track so as to keep the entrants always in sight. The patrol judges are charged with the responsibility of reporting any untoward behavior during the race by either horse or jockey. Before the results of the race are declared official by the placing judges, they receive and study the reports from the patrol judges.

Picking up weight A horse that is carrying more weight than he carried in his last race is picking up weight.

Placing judge The men with the best seats in the house are the placing judges. They determine the identity of the first four horses across the finish line. They also serve as a court before which complaints related to the running of the race are heard.

Plater A claiming horse.

Punter Horse player (common term in England).

Quarter crack A split in the hoof of a horse.

Racing secretary In addition to the responsibilities of the racing secretary that have been discussed in this book, he is responsible for planning the races and issuing the Condition Book, for accepting entrants and stakes, accounting for jockey's fees, for the published program, and for the administrative end of claims.

Rider Jockey; used by paddock judges, as in "Riders Up!" direction to jockeys.

Ring bone Bony enlargement atop hoof or near the pastern bones.

Roarer A horse who coughs in deep and prolonged fashion when galloping.

Route race A mile or longer race.

Running out The tendency of a horse to run wide on turns, thereby losing time by racing a longer actual distance.

Sand crack Crack in the wall of the hoof running downward from the coronet to the ground.

Sesamoiditis Inflammation of the bones above and behind the fetlock joint.

Silks Jockey's riding uniform.

Sire Stallion kept for breeding.

Snip A small patch on the horse's lip or nose. Sometimes it is white; sometimes, flesh-colored.

Splint Bony growth on the side of the splint bone.

Sprint race A race of seven furlongs or less.

Stallion Male horse kept for breeding purposes.

Star Small patch of white hair on the horse's forehead.

Starter The man in charge of the process of getting the horses into the starting gate and officially starting the race.

Steward The highest tribunal at a racing meeting, save the state racing commission itself, are the stewards. One steward is appointed by the State Racing Commission, another by the Jockey Club, and a third by the track. These three men are empowered to determine the arrangements for the conduct of the racing meeting, to regulate the personnel at the track, to judge claims of fouls, and to investigate on their own initiative a suspicion of foul. In addition, they hear and rule on the complaints and problems of jockeys and their agents, and of owners and trainers.

Stripe Thin mark running down the horse's face to the bridge of his nose or below.

Tack Riding equipment, such as the bridle and saddle.

Track take The amount of money taken by the track as its share of the wagered money in the pari-mutuel. The track take is removed, the state's share is removed, and what's left over is divided amongst the holders of winning tickets.

Turf Generally, the race course; specifically, the grass racing oval inside the dirt course.

Walking ring The oval near the paddock, around which the horses walk after having been saddled and in which they are mounted by their jockeys.

Weighing in The process wherein a jockey, at the completion of the race, is weighed in order to determine whether he "lost" too much weight during the race. On days when the track is not muddy, he is not expected to lose in excess of two pounds.

Weighing out The process wherein a jockey is weighed prior to a race to determine whether his weight is within the total weight assigned his mount. Overweight is made known to the public. Overweight, however, is limited to five pounds.

Whistler A horse that emits a whistling sound as a result of strain on the lungs and respiratory system.

Wind sucker Horse that swallows air while racing.

LEADING STABLES—MONEY WON (1978)

Owner	Sts.	1st	2nd	3rd	Purses
Harbor View Farm	362	64	51	40	$2,097,443
Elmendorf	541	74	75	72	1,732,605
Sommer, S.	639	111	106	73	1,505,853
Tartan Stable	478	56	61	69	1,270,943
Greentree Stable	145	45	33	21	1,196,849
Calumet Farm	119	33	19	20	1,065,951
Hunt, N.B.	385	50	44	40	1,053,563
Farish, W. S. III	341	55	50	47	861,743
Stafford Farm.	287	54	47	37	780,074
Levesque, J.L.	316	51	46	58	778,949
Hawksworth Farm	276	73	42	42	759,233
Hooper, F.W.	414	43	49	54	743,651
Lasater, D.	474	78	72	59	719,379
Hickory Tree Stable	126	33	22	20	667,557
Pinetree Stable	152	23	28	16	662,665

LEADING STABLES—RACES WON (1978)

Owner	Sts.	1st	2nd	3rd	Purses
Baird, Dale	1,127	162	140	156	$ 309,685
Hillview Farm	729	121	89	71	248,916
Sommer, S.	639	111	106	73	1,505,853
Maxwell, O. C. & P.	604	104	104	97	375,931
Baer, S. M.	598	80	81	80	647,960
Lasater, D.	474	78	72	59	719,379
Monarch Stable Inc.	429	76	70	49	310,368
Elmendorf	541	74	75	72	1,732,605
Meadows, G.	621	74	66	80	140,234
Hawksworth Farm	276	73	42	42	759,233
Dorignac, J. P. Jr.	352	69	59	34	455,907
Mercer, H. P.	304	68	53	42	217,045
The Little Stable	285	67	49	44	314,758
Harbor View Farm	362	64	51	40	2,097,443
Williams, J. C.	396	63	36	45	120,438

LEADING TRAINERS—MONEY WON (1978)

Trainer	Sts.	1st	2nd	3rd	Purses
Barrera, Lazaro S.	592	100	92	75	$3,314,564
Whittingham, Charles	367	63	56	53	2,286,933
Delp, Grover G.	1,045	239	188	170	1,711,330
Leatherbury, King T.	1,486	304	234	177	1,512,048
Martin, Frank	638	112	107	72	1,509,500
Johnson, Phillip G.	417	65	59	61	1,465,931
Dutrow, Richard E.	1,251	223	217	188	1,415,767
Frankel, Robert	563	105	105	81	1,392,081
McAnally, Ronald	429	67	63	54	1,334,300
Kelly, Thomas J.	351	63	46	50	1,322,612
Stephens, Woodford C.	253	55	31	29	1,266,608
Jones, Gary	455	96	64	49	1,232,173
Rettele, Loren	439	62	74	54	1,218,807
Carroll, Del W.	470	75	78	70	1,198,938
Van Berg, Jack C.	555	80	57	69	1,175,438

LEADING TRAINERS—RACES WON (1978)

Trainer	Sts.	1st	2nd	3rd	Purses
Leatherbury, King, T.	1,486	304	234	117	$1,512,048
Hammond, Everett	1,671	295	271	234	849,394
Delp, Grover, G.	1,045	239	188	170	1,711,330
Baird, Dale	1,707	229	213	229	444,146
Dutrow, Richard E.	1,251	223	217	188	1,415,767
Mercer, Henry P.	683	146	106	103	445,833
Williams, J. C.	803	146	94	96	245,723
Hammond, Jerry	731	143	100	102	424,747
Garcia, Juan	576	137	76	90	341,037
Martinez, Raul	694	137	94	85	361,505
Hazelton, Richard P.	776	135	110	98	851,940
Hough, Stanley M.	686	134	111	88	799,703
Spurling, Wayne A.	691	113	82	82	251,634
Martin, Frank	638	112	107	72	1,509,500
Delahoussaye, Harold	584	109	74	69	460,098

LEADING JOCKEYS—MONEY WON (1978)

Jockey	Mts.	1st	2nd	3rd	Pct.	Purses
McHargue, D. G.	1,762	375	294	263	.213	$6,188,353
Velasquez, J.	1,603	304	230	227	.190	5,364,921
Cordero, A. Jr.	1,306	234	198	208	.179	5,320,503
†Shoemaker, W.	1,245	271	194	156	.218	5,231,390
Cauthen, S.	1,402	209	224	187	.149	4,509,704
Fell, J.	1,783	311	272	213	.174	4,397,390
Pincay, L Jr.	1,428	287	253	205	.201	4,132,993
Delahoussaye, E.	1,666	384	285	238	.230	3,345,789
Cruguet, J.	1,224	200	169	166	.163	3,252,201
Toro, F.	1,219	160	174	185	.131	2,986,036
Hernandez, R.	996	172	130	145	.173	2,910,556
Hawley, S.	1,338	360	255	164	.269	2,877,920
Maple, E.	929	140	146	126	.151	2,653,408
McCarron, C. J.	1,304	197	203	160	.151	2,546,470
Pierce, D.	970	116	114	119	.120	2,538,316

LEADING JOCKEYS—RACES WON (1978)

Jockey	Mts.	1st	2nd	3rd	Pct.	Purses
Delahoussaye, E.	1,666	384	285	238	.230	$3,345,789
McHargue, D. G.	1,762	375	294	263	.213	6,188,353
Hawley, S.	1,338	360	255	164	.269	2,877,920
Fell, J.	1,783	311	272	213	.174	4,397,390
Velasquez, J.	1,603	304	230	227	.190	5,364,921
Pincay, L Jr.	1,428	287	253	205	.201	4,132,993
Neff, S.	1,831	276	224	215	.151	517,241
Bracciale, V. Jr.	1,300	275	216	204	.212	2,468,272
*Kupfer, T.	1,788	275	278	251	.154	1,896,026
†Shoemaker, W.	1,245	271	194	156	.218	5,231,390
*Franklin, R. J.	1,274	262	233	207	.206	1,756,950
Catalano, W.	1,298	256	206	157	.197	1,406,417
Gall, D.	1,338	253	212	206	.189	652,773
Romero, R. P.	1,418	242	212	149	.171	925,339
Macbeth, D.	1,617	237	234	207	.147	2,372,892

Scale of Weights for Age

Distance	Age	Jan	Feb	Mar	Apr	May	Jun	Jul	Aug	Sep	Oct	Nov	Dec
½ m.	2 yrs	x	x	x	x	x	x	x	105	108	111	114	114
	3 yrs	117	117	119	119	121	123	125	126	127	128	129	129
	4 yrs	130	130	130	130	130	130	130	130	130	130	130	130
	5 yrs & up	130	130	130	130	130	130	130	130	130	130	130	130
¾ m.	2 yrs	x	x	x	x	x	x	x	102	105	108	111	111
	3 yrs	114	114	117	117	119	121	123	125	126	127	128	128
	4 yrs	129	129	130	130	130	130	130	130	130	130	130	130
	5 yrs & up	130	130	130	130	130	130	130	130	130	130	130	130
1 m.	2 yrs	x	x	x	x	x	x	x	x	96	99	102	102
	3 yrs	107	107	111	111	113	115	117	119	121	122	123	123
	4 yrs	127	127	128	128	127	126	126	126	126	126	126	126
	5 yrs & up	128	128	128	128	127	126	126	126	126	126	126	126
1¼ m.	2 yrs	x	x	x	x	x	x	x	x	x	x	x	x
	3 yrs	101	101	107	107	111	113	116	118	120	121	122	122
	4 yrs	125	125	127	127	127	126	126	126	126	126	126	126
	5 yrs & up	127	127	127	127	127	127	126	126	126	126	126	126

	x	x	x	x	x	x	x	x	x	x	x	x
1½ m. 2 yrs		98	98	104	104	108	111	114	117	119	121	122	122
3 yrs		124	124	126	126	126	126	126	126	126	126	126	126
4 yrs		126	126	126	126	126	126	126	126	126	126	126	126
5 yrs & up		126	126	126	126	126	126	126	126	126	126	126	126
2 m. 3 yrs		96	96	102	102	106	109	112	114	117	119	120	120
4 yrs		124	124	126	126	126	126	126	125	125	124	124	124
5 yrs		126	126	126	126	126	126	126	125	125	124	124	124

In all races except handicaps and races in which the conditions expressly state to the contrary, two-year-old fillies get sex allowance of 3 pounds and three-year-old fillies and mares 5 pounds before September 1st, and 3 pounds thereafter.

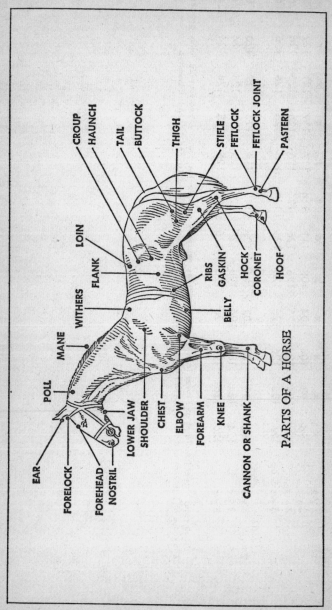

PARTS OF A HORSE